*TWAYNE'S WORLD AUTHORS SERIES*
*A Survey of the World's Literature*


# RUSSIA


Charles Moser, George Washington University
EDITOR

# Alexander  Solzhenitsyn

**TWAS 479**

Alexander  Solzhenitsyn

# ALEXANDER SOLZHENITSYN

### By ANDREJ KODJAK
*New York University*

## TWAYNE PUBLISHERS
A DIVISION OF G. K. HALL & CO., BOSTON

**Library of Congress Cataloging in Publication Data**

Kodjak, Andrej, 1926–
 Alexander Solzhenitsyn.

 (Twayne's world authors series ; TWAS 479 : Russia)
 Bibliography: p. 165-66
 Includes index.
 1. Solzhenitsyn, Aleksandr Isaevich, 1918–
—Criticism and interpretation.
PG3488.04Z72       891.7'3'44       77-20681
ISBN  0-8057-6320-1

# *Contents*

# *About the Author*

Andrej Kodjak is an Associate Professor of Slavic Languages and Literatures and Chairman of the Slavic Department at New York University. Born in Prague, Czechoslovakia, to a Russian family which left Russia after the Civil War, he studied Theology and Philology in Prague, Paris, Montreal (M.A. 1957), New York (B.D. 1959), and Philadelphia (Ph.D. 1963).

Professor Kodjak, prior to his position at NYU, taught Russian Language and Russian Literature at the University of Pennsylvania and at Vanderbilt University. He conducted research in methods of teaching the Russian Language and in the literature of Alexander Pushkin. His works on Pushkin are published in the *American Contributions to the Seventh International Congress of Slavicists* and in *Alexander Puškin — A Symposium on the 175th Anniversary of His Birth*. In recent years, Professor Kodjak has also been engaged in the structural analysis of literature. This method is applied to the works of Solzhenitsyn in the present volume.

# *Preface*

The critic who approaches the works of any living author is inevitably at a certain disadvantage because of his proximity to his subject. First of all, the fact that the author is still writing makes a critical summary of his production impossible and creates serious difficulties in evaluating individual elements as well as the aggregate of his works. An additional difficulty is a certain lack of objectivity. Historical, political, and sociological conditions affect both the writer under study and the critic, so that the latter may find it difficult to decide whether his reactions are sparked by the works of the writer or by those contemporary conditions. Some subjectivity in any study of a contemporary author is thus almost unavoidable. Finally, one must remember that the closer in time one stands to an event, the less accessible are documents, memoirs, and private correspondence and the less objective is the information that is available.

All these disadvantages weighed heavily upon me while I was preparing this book. Although I have been fortunate enough not to have lived under Stalin's regime, my upbringing among Russian émigrés in Prague made me very much aware of the recent tragic events in the USSR. Thus although I have attempted to preserve maximum objectivity, a subjective perception of Solzhenitsyn's works can easily be detected in this study. The lack of documentation on both Solzhenitsyn's life and the Stalinist era causes great difficulty for the scholar: the most precious ingredient for a literary researcher — the minute details reflecting the texture of both the writer's life and his epoch — remains in Solzhenitsyn's case virtually inaccessible to the Western student.

Finally, Solzhenitsyn embarked upon his literary career only two decades ago. He is a prolific writer; his literary plans are extensive; and one may expect him to continue publishing. Thus, any comprehensive evaluation of his art and philosophy at this point must be quite tentative, for his future works may reflect new and different features and ideas. All these factors lead me to present this study as merely a modest introduction to the first period of Solzhenitsyn's career, i.e., the period that he spent on the soil of his homeland, on the assumption that a second period will follow in his exile.

Solzhenitsyn is admired by many people in the USSR as well as in the West primarily for three reasons: for his bold stand against a powerful, totalitarian government, for his political ideas, and for his artistic achievements. Although these three are closely inter-related, I have written this book primarily about Solzhenitsyn the author, dealing with other aspects of his life only when necessary for a better understanding of his works. It is not their current political impact upon us today, but rather their literary merit which will determine how future generations will evaluate him as a writer. Thus this book treats Solzhenitsyn mainly as an artist living in a turbulent epoch in Russian history.

It is my belief that Solzhenitsyn's works are well-functioning sys-tems containing interacting signs which acquire their full meaning only when viewed in a total context. Thus each work must be per-ceived singly and wholly; the reader must bear its interrelated signs simultaneously in mind. Such a reading cannot be achieved at once. It requires careful analysis, the initial stage of which may be found in this study.

Indeed, Solzhenitsyn's system of interrelated signs is so rich that an analysis of them would require a volume exceeding the works themselves in size. I have, therefore, selected only the most signifi-cant signs for this study, leaving the remainder for the reader to dis-cover. It is my belief that the very process of recognizing meaning-ful interrelations of dispersed signs in a work of art is a necessary step in its understanding, and is the most exciting, rewarding, and pleasurable part of reading. Consequently, I have given the reader an opportunity to exercise his ingenuity at discovering other rela-tionships. In order to help the reader judge whether selected signs really do interact with other signs and thus function in the structure of the work, I have quoted directly from Solzhenitsyn's prose as frequently as is helpful. By doing so, I hoped to acquaint the reader more closely with both the author's style and structure, as well as they can be transmitted in translation.

One must remember, however, that Solzhenitsyn's major novels were written for publication in the Soviet Union and had to under-go the censors' scrutiny. Such topics as the primacy of spiritual over material values, the interruption of the nation's cultural tradi-tion, and the apocalyptic confrontation of man with the naked bru-tality of Stalinism could not be openly discussed in any work submitted for publication in the USSR. Therefore, the Western reader must examine Solzhenitsyn's works with a magnifying glass even stronger than that used by the Soviet censors.

The Western reader of Russian literature faces certain persisting difficulties. One of them is the names of the characters, especially in a larger work such as a novel. In this book I have tried to reduce the complexity of Russian names by using in most cases a character's surname only. I have also simplified the multitude of abbreviations for the Soviet secret police. There are eight different names for that institution, from Lenin's VChK to the contemporary KGB. For this book I have chosen the abbreviation MGB (Ministry of State Security), the name of the secret police from 1946 to 1953, the years in which Solzhenitsyn's fiction is primarily set.

ANDREJ KODJAK

*New York University*

# Acknowledgments

I express my sincere gratitude to my editors, Linda Myers and Adele Barker, and to the publishers who have graciously permitted me to quote from the following:

*Alexander Solzhenitsyn: Critical Essays and Documentary Materials,* John B. Dunlop, Richard Haugh, Alexis Klimoff, eds., Belmont, Mass.: Nordland Publishing Co., 1973.

Alexander Solzhenitsyn, *Nobel Lecture,* F.D. Reeve, trans., Farrar, Straus and Girous, 1972.

Alexander Solzhenitsyn, *Stories and Prose Poems,* Michael Glenny, trans., Farrar, Straus and Giroux, 1970.

Alexander Solzhenitsyn, *One Day in the Life of Ivan Denisovich,* R. Hingley and M. Hayward, trans., Bantam, New York, 1963.

Alexander Solzhenitsyn, *Cancer Ward,* Nicholas Bethell and David Burg, trans., Bantam, New York, 1969.

Alexander Solzhenitsyn, *The Love-Girl and The Innocent,* Nicholas Bethell and David Burg, trans., Bantam, New York, 1971.

Alexander Solzhenitsyn, *August 1914,* Michael Glenny, trans., Bantam, New York, 1974.

Alexander Solzhenitsyn, *The First Circle,* Thomas P. Whitney, trans., Harper & Row, New York, 1968.

Alexander Solzhenitsyn, *The Gulag Archipelago,* Thomas P. Whitney, trans., Harper & Row, 1973.

George Kennan, "Between Earth and Hell," *The New York Review of Books,* 1974.

# Chronology

1918 Born December 11 in Kislovodsk.
1936 Graduates from secondary school in Rostov-on-Don.
1937 Enters the University of Rostov-on-Don, Department of Physics and Mathematics.
1939 Enrolls concurrently in a correspondence program at the Institute of History, Philosophy, and Literature in Moscow.
1941 Graduates from the University of Rostov-on-Don.
1941-1942 Serves in the Red Army as a driver of horse-drawn vehicles.
1942 Completes an abridged course in the artillery school in November.
November 1942-February 1945 — Serves as a battery commander.
1945 Arrested by counter-intelligence in February. Sentenced on July 7 to eight years in a labor camp.
1945-1946 Serves time in a correctional labor camp.
1946-1950 Serves time in a "special prison," a scientific research institute near Moscow.
1950-1953 Serves time in a "special camp" in Ekibastuz, Kazakhstan.
1953 Released from labor camp on March 5 and exiled to Central Asia.
1953-1956 Teaches mathematics and physics in a secondary school in exile.
1954 Undergoes a second treatment for cancer in Tashkent.
1956 Rehabilitated.
1957 Returns to European Russia. Continues teaching.
1961 Sends manuscript of *One Day in the Life of Ivan Denisovich* to the literary magazine *Novy mir,* in November. Meets the chief editor of *Novy mir,* Alexander Tvardovsky, in December.
1962 *One Day in the Life of Ivan Denisovich* published in *Novy mir* in November.
1963 Three short stories, "Matryona's Homestead," "An Incident at Krechetovka Station," and "For the Good of the

Cause," published in *Novy mir.* Begins work on *The Cancer Ward,* considered in autumn for publication by *Novy mir.*

1964   Candidacy for Lenin Prize defeated in April. In spring Tvardovsky reads an abridged version (eighty-seven chapters out of ninety-six) of *The First Circle. The First Circle* discussed by the editorial board of *Novy mir* on June 11. Manuscript of *The First Circle* sent to the West in October.

1965   Manuscripts and private archives confiscated by the secret police on September 11. Sends letter of protest.

1966   *The Cancer Ward* discussed by the editorial board of *Novy mir* on June 18. In July sends letter of protest against persecution to Brezhnev. Open discussion of *The Cancer Ward* organized by the Writer's Union on November 16.

1967   Completes the first two parts of an autobiographical work *A Calf Was Butting an Oak* in April and November respectively. Sends an open letter to the Fourth Congress of Soviet Writers on May 16. On September 12 sends a letter to the Secretariat of the Writers' Union. Meets with the Secretariat on September 22. On December 1 sends a letter to the Secretariat of the Writers' Union demanding action on his behalf.

1968   Excerpts from *The Cancer Ward* published by *The London Times Literary Supplement* on April 11. On April 25 sends a letter to *Le Monde, Unita,* and *Literaturnaya gazeta* protesting the unauthorized printing of excerpts from *The Cancer Ward* abroad. Publication in English of *The First Circle* in September and *The Cancer Ward* in October.

1969   Expelled from the local chapter of the Writers' Union in Ryazan on November 4 and from the Writers' Union of RSFSR on November 5. Sends a letter to the Secretariat of the Writers' Union protesting expulsion on November 12. On November 30 attacked in an article published in *Literaturnaya gazeta* suggesting his deportation from the USSR.

1970   Announced as the winner of the Nobel Prize for Literature on October 9. On November 27 decides not to go to Stockholm to receive it. Awarded the Nobel Prize *in absentia* on December 10.

1971   Authorizes the publication in Russian of the first part of a trilogy *August 1914* in Paris in May.

1972   Writes a letter to Patriarch Pimen of Russia in March. Grants an interview to correspondents from *The New York Times* and *The Washington Post* on March 30.

1973    On August 23 the secret police receive information as to the whereabouts of a copy of *The Gulag Archipelago.* Grants an interview to the Associated Press and *Le Monde* on the same day. Sends a 13,000-word letter to the Soviet leaders on September 5. Contacted by the secret police on September 24 through his divorced wife, Natalya Reshetovskaya. *The Gulag Archipelago* (Part I) published in Russian in Paris on December 28.

1973-1974 Writes three articles (published in a collection of articles by Soviet dissidents under the title *From Under the Rubble,* Paris, 1974).

1974    Grants interview to a correspondent of *Time* magazine in January. Appeals to Russian youth through the underground press in the beginning of 1974 in an essay entitled "Don't Live a Lie." Arrested in Moscow on February 12. Deported to West Germany on February 13.

## CHAPTER 1

# Citizen and Writer

## I  Early Years, War, and Exile

THE life of Alexander Isaevich Solzhenitsyn, winner of the Nobel Prize for Literature in 1970, could be schematized as a curve winding in sharp turns from one extreme to another. The extremes are persecution and success, poverty and wealth, imprisonment and freedom, peril and security. Solzhenitsyn grew up without a father in very modest circumstances but received an excellent education. An outstanding artillery officer in World War II, he was arrested for criticizing Stalin, who ruled the very country Solzhenitsyn was fighting to defend. After serving out his term in various labor camps, he lived in obscurity until the publication of his first novel, which suddenly made him the most prominent living Russian writer. Later, the Union of Soviet Writers ostracized him, and his books have been banned in his own country. Though he was under attack at home, the West acknowledged his artistic merits by awarding him the Nobel Prize for Literature in 1970. While his books were widely published in the West, he lived under constant harassment and without a steady income in his homeland. Then, following his sudden arrest, he found himself in Western Europe, free, in a position to collect his considerable royalties, yet exiled from his own country.

These unique contrasts constitute merely the facade of Solzhenitsyn's life. Behind that facade lies his unshakable devotion to his art, to his convictions, and to his nation. Now, after the first period of his literary career in his native country has ended, his future may be more tranquil. This first period of Solzhenitsyn's life is the subject of this chapter.

Solzhenitsyn's biography, as the term is commonly understood in literary studies, scarcely exists. The very meager available data reflect exclusively the externals of his life and do not refer to his

15

relationships with his family and friends; they omit all the complex of details necessary for an in-depth portrait of a man. Solzhenitsyn's singular position in contemporary literature is due to the unusual conditions under which he lived and wrote until his expulsion from the USSR on February 13, 1974. The Soviet regime made it virtually impossible for literary scholars to correspond with him, to interview him, or to examine his first drafts, notebooks, or diaries. Solzhenitsyn is thus known to us almost exclusively through his literary works and his public statements. We must be content with the few autobiographical details we can gather from his fictional works and with his public statements and letters addressed to various Soviet governmental agencies, in particular the Union of Soviet Writers.

In all fairness, one must add that Solzhenitsyn's personal distaste for publicity has also made it difficult to obtain information about his private life. He seems to wish to divorce the image of the artist from the private man, and to appear before the public exclusively in the former capacity. Nevertheless, a modest attempt at summarizing his biography is justified since the major events in his life have significantly influenced his artistic production and since, likewise, his literary work has strongly affected his personal destiny.

Alexander Solzhenitsyn was born on December 11, 1918, in Kislovodsk, a spa in the Caucasian Mountains. His father was an educated man. According to Solzhenitsyn's autobiography submitted to the Nobel Foundation in 1970, his father left his studies in philology at Moscow University in order to volunteer for the Russian Army in 1914. Solzehnitsyn was born after his father died and thus grew up as an orphan (in the Russian sense of the word).[1] Mother and son then moved to a larger city — Rostov-on-Don — where she worked as a typist and stenographer to support herself and her only child. Solzhenitsyn grew up here, attended the university, and embarked on his first literary efforts — which, in his autobiography, he dismisses as the "usual adolescent nonsense."[2]

As a student, Solzhenitsyn sought to pursue his literary interests, but as Rostov University did not offer the program he wanted and a move to Moscow at that time was financially impossible, he took up mathematics in 1937. He found it easy, and — perhaps precisely because the program failed to challenge him sufficiently — he enrolled from 1939-41 in a correspondence program of the prestigious Moscow Institute of History, Philosophy, and Literature. In his first year at the university, Solzhenitsyn was assigned a paper on a historical topic: the so-called "Samsonov Debacle" of 1914. It was then that he began to collect information and materials on Russia's role in the First World War, which only much later, in 1971, appeared in book form as *August 14*. (August 1914).

Before Solzhenitsyn enlisted in the army in 1941, he apparently lived an intellectually active but socially isolated life. As the son of a widow who earned her money by the tedious work of typing during a time of general economic hardship in the Soviet Union, the young Solzhenitsyn was doubtless obliged to carry out many domestic duties. Nevertheless, he had graduated from secondary school with excellent marks and so in 1937 had received a Stalin scholarship at the university, in recognition of high achievement. While at Rostov University, he met and married Natalya Reshetovskaya, a chemistry student.

Solzhenitsyn's professional training at the university served him well during the war and later in the labor camps. Because of his knowledge of mathematics, he was sent to artillery school and rose to the rank of captain in the army. We know little about Solzhenitsyn's life during the war except for a brief official note in the document of rehabilitation issued him by the Supreme Court of the USSR on February 6, 1956:

From Solzhenitsyn's military record and a report by Captain Melnikov, who served with him, it is clear that from 1942 until the time of his arrest Solzhenitsyn served on several fronts of the Great Fatherland War, fought courageously for his homeland, more than once displayed personal heroism and inspired the devotion of the section he commanded. Solzhenitsyn's section was the best in the unit for discipline and battle effectiveness.[3]

At the front Solzhenitsyn found two important ties with the past. As it happened, he saw action on precisely the same territory where his father had fought during the First World War and where General Samsonov's military catastrophe, which Solzhenitsyn had studied at Rostov University, took place.

Solzhenitsyn encountered a second link with his past in the person of Nikolai Vitkevich, a friend from secondary school and Rostov University, who served on the same front. They exchanged letters, sometimes containing candid views on political issues, including Stalin's conduct of the war. Solzhenitsyn and Vitkevich's close friendship of eighteen years, from 1927 to 1945, was tragically broken off by their arrest and long years of imprisonment occasioned by the interception of their letters. Solzhenitsyn was taken to Moscow's famous prison, Lyubyanka, and in July 1945, was sentenced to eight years in a labor camp. His friend Vitkevich, then in an army prison, was sentenced to ten years in a camp.

In the autobiography Solzhenitsyn submitted to the Nobel Foundation, he speaks briefly of the years spent in concentration camps, prisons, and forced exile in connection with his literary works:

At first I served my sentence in corrective-labor camps of a mixed type (as described in the play *The Love-Girl and the Innocent*). Later, in 1946, I was summoned from there as a mathematician into the system of scientific research institutes of the MVD-MGB and in such "special prisons" (see *The First Circle*) spent the middle part of my sentence. In 1950 I was sent to the newly-established *special* camps for political prisoners only. In such a camp in the town of Ekibastuz in Kazakhstan (see *One Day in the Life of Ivan Denisovich*) I worked as a common laborer, a bricklayer, and a foundryman. There I developed a malignant tumor which was operated on but not cured: its true nature was discovered only later.

With a delay of one month past the end of my eight-year term there arrived — without any new sentence or even a "resolution of the OSO" — an administrative order: I was not to be freed but sent into PERPETUAL EXILE in Kok-Terek (southern Kazakhstan). This was not a special measure directed at me but a very common procedure at the time.[4]

His rehabilitation, like others, was a politically significant event — a clear and direct attempt by Khrushchev's government to de-Stalinize the USSR. The fresh breeze of liberalism, limited though it was, created a new climate throughout the entire country. It engendered aspirations for a better future, but it also simultaneously created an open gulf between those who welcomed liberalization and those who wished to preserve the foundations of Stalinism. Thus two basic factions — the liberals and the conservatives — clashed, sometimes openly, sometimes covertly, but always unceasingly. This split presumably began even before Stalin's death and became more evident under the new government dominated by the "conservatives" Georgi Malenkov, Vyacheslav Molotov, and Lavrenti Beria. These disciples of the Stalinist hard line were, however, removed from key positions in a struggle which lasted from 1953 to 1956 and which ended with the emergence of a new leader, Nikita Khrushchev, a "liberal" statesman in the context of the post-Stalinist USSR.

Khrushchev delivered his famous speech exposing Stalin's tyranny to a closed session of the Twentieth Party Congress in 1956. This defamation of Stalin by Khrushchev and his supporters in front of an audience which included many who had, to at least some degree, approved of and participated in the former administration, was extremely bold. The risk this move entailed is demonstrated by the fact that Khrushchev's condemnation of Stalin was made public only five years later — in October, 1961. at the Twenty-second Party Congress. At that time the removal of Stalin's body from the Lenin Mausoleum on Red Square, the renaming of streets, factories, and collective farms, and the change of the name of the city of Stalingrad to Volgograd were designed to symbolize the regime's break with Stalinist practice.

Khrushchev's open denunciation of Stalin was doubtless a major factor in Solzhenitsyn's decision to publish his first work, *Odin den' Ivana Denisovicha (One Day in the Life of Ivan Denisovich).* The manuscript reached the desk of Alexander Tvardovsky, a leading Russian poet and chief editor of the most prominent liberal journal in the USSR, *Novy mir* (New World). It is said that Tvardovsky, who knew Khrushchev personally, took the manuscript to the premier and obtained his direct approval to publish it. *One Day in the Life of Ivan Denisovich* appeared in the November issue of *Novy mir* for 1962 and became one of the tools Khrushchev used to expose Stalin's tyranny.

In the first issue of *Novy mir* for 1963, two of Solzhenitsyn's stories appeared: "Matrenin dvor" (Matryona's Homestead) and "Sluchai na stantsii Krechetovka" (An Incident at Krechetovka Station). "Dlia pol'zy dela" (For the Good of the Cause) was published in the seventh issue of that year. Solzhenitsyn published in the Soviet Union mainly during the few months from November, 1962 to July, 1963. Only one article appeared in 1965, in *Literaturnaya gazeta (The Literary Gazette),* published by the Union of Soviet Writers, and "Zakhar-Kalita" (Zakhar the Pouch), far from his most significant story, appeared in the first issue of *Novy mir* for 1966. From 1964 on Solzhenitsyn's works began appearing outside the USSR both in Russian and in translations. His major novels, *Rakovyi Korpus (The Cancer Ward)* and *V Kruge pervom (The First Circle),* two dramas — *Olen' i shalashovka* (The Love-Girl And The Innocent) and *Svecha na vetru* (The Candle in the Wind) — and his unfinished works *August 1914* and *Arkhipelag Gulag (The Gulag Archipelago),* were published outside the USSR and remain legally inaccessible to the Soviet reader.

It is important to keep in mind that Solzhenitsyn's works published in the USSR appeared for the most part before mid-1963. This fact reflects the political struggle between Stalin's followers and the less dogmatic forces associated to a certain extent with Khrushchev's policies. The outcome of this conflict was Khrushchev's forced retirement on October 15, 1964, not long after the last of Solzhenitsyn's major works were published in the USSR. Thus Solzhenitsyn's literary career and his personal fate were closely connected with Khrushchev's efforts at de-Stalinization.

With the change in the political climate in the USSR, some literary critics began to attack Solzhenitsyn. *One Day in the Life of Ivan Denisovich* and the short story, "Matryona's Homestead" were vigorously criticized. Most of the accusers claimed that Ivan Denisovich was not representative of the new Soviet man and that Matryona was a religious anachronism in the new, "progressive" Soviet society.

Eventually Solzhenitsyn himself became a target of criticism by various party dignitaries, and as a result his status as a writer and as a private citizen in the Soviet Union was seriously threatened. Nevertheless, he decided to stand by his principles, to insist on his right to speak freely and to write truthfully. The result was an extraordinary confrontation between a single courageous man and one of the most powerful governments in the world.

## II   *From Fame to Exile*

Several significant events occurred in the ten-year period between 1963, when Solzhenitsyn was at the peak of his literary career in the USSR, and February 1974, when he was arrested in Moscow and deported to West Germany. During this decade Solzhenitsyn both received world-wide acclaim as a Nobel Prize winner, and experienced the humiliation of arrest and expulsion from his homeland. These ten years are particularly pertinent to this study, for it was during this time that he made several political statements which have deepened our understanding of him as a man and as a writer.

The first direct blow against Solzhenitsyn came from the powerful Union of Soviet Writers, membership in which is virtually required if one is to publish in the USSR. The Union did not invite Solzhenitsyn to attend the Fourth All-Union Writers' Congress in 1967, although as a member he had every right to attend, if not as a delegate, then certainly as a guest. This slight would probably have gone unnoticed had Solzhenitsyn not reacted by composing a seven-page letter to the presidium of the congress and mailing copies to each of the 250 delegates several days in advance of the meeting. When the congress convened on May 18, the vast majority of the delegates had read Solzhenitsyn's letter. Thus he created a forum for himself within the framework of a well-organized state institution — no small achievement in a controlled society.

The first part of the letter consists of two proposals of general importance:

> I propose that the Congress adopt a resolution which would demand and ensure the abolition of all censorship, open or hidden, of all fictional writing, and which would release publishing houses from the obligation to obtain authorization for the publication of every printed page.
>
> I propose that all guarantees for the defence of Union members subjected to slander and unjust persecution be clearly formulated in Paragraph 22 of the Union statutes, so that past illegalities will not be repeated.[5]

In the second half of his letter, Solzhenitsyn demands that the Union defend him against the slander directed at him for the past three years, including the false accusation that he betrayed his country during the Second World War. He also asks the Union to defend him against the unfair suppression of his plays, film scenarios, and recitations on radio and for special audiences.

The vigor and passion with which Solzhenitsyn began his crusade to liberate literature from state censorship may surprise the Western reader. It is well to remember, however, that Russians regard literature, not just as a source of entertainment or aesthetic pleasure, but rather as an open forum for the most serious discussion of social ills, the destiny of the nation, and the goals and aspirations of their nation and mankind. Thus without a free and honest literature, the Russians and other nationalities in the Soviet Union lack the opportunity to discuss and, by extension, to think creatively about their past and future, and to shape their own destiny.[6] In this context, Solzhenitsyn's letter becomes extremely significant, and one can more easily appreciate the dimensions of the scandal he created by mailing copies of the letter to the delegates to the congress.

Space does not permit an analysis of all the ramifications of Solzhenitsyn's bold move. The congress discussed none of his proposals, although many delegates supported his letter with their own statements.

Needless to say, the attacks on Solzhenitsyn did not subside after 1967. In 1969 — after the publication abroad of *The Cancer Ward* and *The First Circle* — the Union of Soviet Writers expelled Solzhenitsyn. He responded with a caustic letter. Ironically, the next year (1970), he won the Nobel Prize for Literature, an event which engendered much furore and controversy. Those who admired Solzhenitsyn's works and his daring stand for freedom and truth received the news jubilantly. The Communist Party of the USSR, however, interpreted the award as politically motivated. In a letter of November, 1970, to the Swedish Academy, Solzhenitsyn stated that he would not travel to Sweden to accept the Nobel Prize for fear the Soviet government might seize that opportunity to exile him by refusing to let him re-enter his country. Nevertheless, he sent the traditional Nobel Lecture (published in 1972), in which he discussed the mission of art — and specifically literature — in the history of individual nations and all mankind.

His thesis here is that art has been given to man as a unique device for recording the experience of one sector of humanity, in a certain time and place, for other nations and for future generations as well. Solzhenitsyn's understanding of art as such is clearly religious. It assumes God's will and initiative in saving humanity from the inevitable cataclysms caused by a lack of communication between generations and nations. In Solzhenitsyn's view, art is the single means of human communication which by its very nature is devoted to truth. Thus art in general and literature in particular are the major vehicles by which accumulated experience is transmitted in an undistorted version transcending the barriers of time and space. Solzhenitsyn considers this particularly important in our age of violence:

> We will be told: What can literature do against the pitiless onslaught of naked violence? Let us not forget that violence does not and cannot flourish by itself; it is inevitably intertwined with LYING. Between them there is the closest, the most profound and natural bond: nothing screens violence except lies, and the only way lies can hold out is by violence. Whoever has once announced violence as his method must inexorably choose lying as his PRINCIPLE.[7]

Given Solzhenitsyn's notion that violence and destruction are closely related to the distortion of truth, the major task of the writer becomes that of using the communicative capacity of art to convey the truth to his fellow man removed from him in time and space.

Meanwhile the campaign against Solzhenitsyn in the Soviet Union was mounting in size, in the gravity of its accusations, and in the frequency of the harassment directed against him and his family. It is not the intention of this study to examine closely allegations which cannot be properly documented or examined. It seems, however, that Solzhenitsyn's life became not merely difficult, but actually endangered. Yet on September 5, 1973, scarcely a year after the publication of his Nobel Lecture in Sweden, Solzhenitsyn sent a 13,000-word letter to the Soviet government *Pis'mo sovetskim vozhdyam* (Letter to the Soviet Leaders) calling for the most radical changes in the ideological, political, administrative, and economic structure of the USSR. His reforms, if enacted, would constitute nothing less than a complete revolution from the top, something that has occurred only once in Russian history: under Peter the Great, at the beginning of the eighteenth century. After Solzhenitsyn's expulsion from the USSR, he made his letter public.[8] Since only six months elapsed between the time he sent his letter to the government and his forced exile, one may conjecture that these two events are related.

Solzhenitsyn states clearly in the introduction to his letter that he does not intend to deal with his country's past, as he has done in his fiction, but rather with her future. He foresees two major threats to the Soviet Union: an ideological war with Marxist China and an environmental cataclysm which will destroy all of Western civilization, including the Soviet Union. In Solzhenitsyn's view, the Soviet Union must completely abandon Marxist doctrine as the official state ideology in order to escape a clash with China, which in his estimation would cost the USSR at least 60 million casualties. The abandonment of Marxist ideology would destroy the messianic drive behind Soviet foreign policy, with its intensive support of revolutionary movements all over the world and its maintenance of post-war territorial gains in Europe. Solzhenitsyn also favors self-determination for all the nations now incorporated in the Soviet Union. Ending its support of so-called "liberation movements," in competition with China, and eliminating its antagonism towards the United States would allow the Soviet government to halt its intensive industrial and urban buildup and to follow a no-growth economic policy. The latter, according to Solzhenitsyn, is the only means of averting the environmental cataclysm which is inevitable given the present policy of the Soviet government. Once the Soviet Union is free of her international political commitments, she can concentrate on the peaceful development of her vast northeastern territory.

Solzhenitsyn's letter was received rather coolly in Western Europe and America. It was labeled a "neoslavophile" document, reminiscent of that Russian intellectual movement of the nineteenth century — Slavophilism — which advocated the independent development of the nation and her isolation from Western influences. This charge, however, requires some modification. The Slavophiles were not so radical as Solzhenitsyn sounds in his letter, and would hardly have been inclined to retreat into the northeastern territory in order there to construct an idyllic, genuinely Russian nation, predominantly rural, ideologically conservative, and ecologically protected. Solzhenitsyn's letter suggests rather a linkage with another intellectual movement of the past — that of the Old Believers, the religious schismatics, with their eschatological interpretation of history and their acute presentiments of the end of the world. Solzhenitsyn's warning of the danger of a Chinese invasion of the Soviet Union and an environmental cataclysm recalls the Old Believers' predictions of the advent of the Antichrist.

The leading dissenter and defender of civil rights in the USSR, Andrey Sakharov, replied to Solzhenitsyn's letter in a written statement of April 14, 1974. Sakharov agreed with Solzhenitsyn as to the desirability of abandoning Marxism as the official Soviet ideology, and seconded Solzhenitsyn's call for the emancipation of all nations within the borders of the USSR and the Soviet bloc. However, Sakharov strongly criticized Solzhenitsyn's isolationism, arguing that no nation today can survive without close cultural, economic, and scientific ties with other nations. In place of Solzhenitsyn's proposal for creating some kind of national reservation in the northeastern territory, Sakharov proposed that the Soviet borders be opened to free and unrestricted travel, which would lead to a full exchange of ideas, economic standards, and scientific research between Soviet citizens and the rest of the world. To date the Soviet government has not replied to Solzhenitsyn's letter except indirectly, in an article which appeared on May 1, 1974, in the *Literaturnaya gazeta* sarcastically commenting on the Solzhenitsyn-Sakharov dialogue.

One must remember that Solzhenitsyn was writing his fictional works under great pressure and increasingly hostile criticism from Soviet authorities and the press. Under these conditions he made an attempt — and a very successful one too — to establish his independence as a writer. He hired a lawyer in Switzerland, and at least some parts of *The Gulag Archipelago* were smuggled out of the USSR to the West to be published when the author deemed it timely. He was, he has said, reluctant to publish this work, since many who supplied him with information are still alive and could be persecuted by the government for collaborating with him. However, after the Soviet police confiscated a copy of the manuscript, Solzhenitsyn ordered his Western representative to publish it. It appeared in Russian in Paris on December 28, 1973.

Once *The Gulag Archipelago* was released in the West, the charges against Solzhenitsyn became increasingly grave. He was accused of treason, was arrested in Moscow on February 12, 1974, and the next day was flown to Frankfort, West Germany, under escort. The Soviet government then allowed Solzhenitsyn's second wife, Natalya Svetlova, their three sons, her son by a former marriage, and her mother to emigrate: on March 29 they flew from Moscow to Zurich, Switzerland, where they were reunited with him.

Very little is known of Solzhenitsyn's family life. Natalya Reshetovskaya, his first wife, divorced him and remarried while Solzhenitsyn was serving his prison term. After his release and rehabilitation, she returned to him, but only for a short time. His complete absorption in his writing apparently created discord that led to their permanent separation.

Solzhenitsyn's expulsion from his homeland will probably prove to be the most significant event in his life. For a writer, contact with the living language of his nation as well as with the thoughts and feelings of his people is usually as essential as daily light is for a painter. Few writers have survived permanent exile or emigration as artists, and many writers view it as the worst fate possible (one need only recall the letter Boris Pasternak sent to Khrushchev pleading to be allowed to stay and die in his homeland).

Whatever may be the consquences of Solzhenitsyn's expulsion from the Soviet Union, his life has altered so dramatically that future literary historians may find it useful to divide his works into two periods: those written in the USSR, and those written in exile. This study treats the first period of his literary career.

## CHAPTER 2

# One Day in the Life of
# Ivan Denisovich

## I  *The Indictment of Stalinism*

S OLZHENITSYN'S first published work, *One Day in the Life of Ivan Denisovich,* remains his best-known novel. The sensation it created when it appeared in *Novy mir* in 1962 was hardly astonishing, since the novel was published only a few years after Khrushchev's exposure of Stalin's personality cult. No literary work published in the USSR had so candidly described life in Stalin's concentration camps, and this aspect of the novel understandably attracted the greatest attention. The book was generally received as the most radical denunciation of Stalin's reign of terror to date. Now, however, over a decade later, one may take a new, more objective look at this novel, and attempt to evaluate it more fully.

*One Day in the Life of Ivan Denisovich* is the story of one man's struggle for physical and spiritual survival. As the title suggests, this is a virtually plotless account of an ordinary day in a typical concentration camp during the Stalinist era. The novel records the routine behind barbed wire from reveille to retreat including the prisoners' meals, work, searches, free time, and their relationships with one another and the authorities. The day Solzhenitsyn depicts is a rather good one: a prisoner often had far worse. It is also clear that the camp the author describes is by no means the worst in existence: the protagonist himself, Ivan Denisovich Shukhov, recalls that life in the Ust-Izhma camp was much harsher.

If any aspect of Shukhov's day seems unbearable, his sensitivity should not be held accountable, for most of the other prisoners from higher social classes are even less well prepared than he to endure the hardships of a labor camp. Neither the cultural refine-

26

ment nor the sensitivities of the Russian intelligentsia, who lack practical skills, have undermined him. Solzhenitsyn's choice of an uneducated peasant as his protagonist is wise. It is scarcely possible to imagine anyone better suited than Shukhov — an ordinary, sturdy, vigorous man accustomed to physical labor — to endure the extremely harsh conditions prevalent in Stalin's concentration camps.

This choice of the protagonist,[1] however, also creates a problem for the author: the form of the narration. It is plain that Ivan Denisovich, though an intelligent man, is nevertheless totally incapable of functioning as the narrator of a lengthy story. Lack of education is not his only handicap. The natural stoicism of a simple man who is loath to appeal to the feelings of his audience would make Shukhov's account a dry, matter-of-fact presentation similar to that of his foreman, Tyurin, who tells his brigade his life story "without pity, like it wasn't about himself."[2]

If Shukhov could not provide an account of his day, a narrator identified with Solzhenitsyn, with his language and the consciousness of an educated man, could not do so either. The Russian reader would not trust such a narrator, for the social barriers between a gifted mathematician with a university education and a barely literate peasant render mutual understanding very difficult. Therefore Solzhenitsyn chose to create an anonymous narrator who, though present on every page of the book, remains unknown to the reader. The narrator is characterized by his antagonism toward the authorities and by his colloquial language, which is permeated with camp jargon. One may conclude that he is a convict of very humble origins, on the same cultural level as Shukhov but of much broader experience, and that he has acquired during his life a knowledge of human nature which enables him to mediate between persons of different cultural backgrounds. He understands Shukhov intuitively, and portrays him without either idealizing or denigrating him. On the other hand, the narrator knows which aspects of Shukhov's personality, and which features of camp life, would be least comprehensible to the educated reader lacking camp experience. The narrator, therefore, becomes also a commentator, whose point of view plays a central role in the novel.

Through the narrator-commentator Solzhenitsyn introduces a dual perspective into the novel. On the one hand, he pictures life in a concentration camp objectively; on the other, he portrays Ivan Denisovich subjectively, from the narrator's viewpoint. Ivan

Denisovich, as the narrator perceives him, is a complex figure: seemingly simple, even primitive in appearance, yet actually quite sophisticated and spiritually sublime. The reader cannot readily discern this dichotomy without a full awareness of the conditions in the camp where the protagonist spends his day. There would be little literary value, however, in depicting life in a camp without presenting Shukhov's personality in depth. Thus both these features of the novel must be analyzed, for only in their interaction do they reveal the central theme. One must, therefore, begin with the basic aspects of camp life necessary for an understanding of the protagonist, who will be analyzed in the second part of this chapter.

Initially the narrator focuses on three major concerns of the typical convict: food, work, and the camp authorities. The narrator begins his account in a systematic, detached manner at 5:00 a.m. on a January day in 1951 in a concentration camp located somewhere in the steppes of Siberia. The day begins in the freezing barracks with the sound of a hammer pounding against a piece of rail. The narrator describes conditions in the camp detail by detail: the early start of the work day in the complete darkness and frost of a Siberian winter night, the cold of the prisoners' barracks, their starvation diet, and the brutality of the authorities.

The theme of food in the camp is introduced at breakfast. During Shukhov's eight years as a prisoner, he has elevated eating to a true art:

> The only good thing about camp gruel was it was usually hot, but what Shukhov had was now quite cold. Even so, he ate it slow and careful like he always did. Mustn't hurry now, even if the roof caught fire. . . .
> The fish was mostly bones. The flesh was boiled off except for bits on the tails and the heads. Not leaving a single scale or speck of flesh on the skeleton, Shukhov crunched and sucked the bones and spit them out on the table. He didn't leave anything — not even the gills or the tail. He ate the eyes too when they were still in place, but when they'd come off and were floating around in the bowl on their own he didn't eat them. The others laughed at him for this.[3]

During lunch the narrator adds a ritualistic dimension to his description of a perpetually hungry man eating. Since Shukhov has finagled several extra bowls of food for his brigade from the kitchen, he has the right to a second portion. He eats his first bowl very slowly, chewing every mouthful thoroughtly, preparing it for the most complete digestion possible. The extent to which the elementary art of eating is psychologically conditioned is demonstrated by the fact that Shukhov, having expected a larger portion of food this time, does not feel so full as he usually does after one bowl of mush. Next he scrapes every single trace of food from the bowl with a piece of bread crust salvaged for the purpose, until the bowl is almost as clean as if it had been washed.

The explanation for this lengthy procedure of eating mush — which nearly imposes the experience on the reader himself — appears in the narrator's remark as Shukhov watches prisoner K-123 eat during a heated discussion with the privileged Caesar about Eisenstein's film *Ivan the Terrible:* "He ate his mush, but there was no taste in his mouth. It was wasted on him."⁴ Shukhov's eating habits are not merely the instinctive adjustments of a consistently undernourished man, but a complete and well-formulated strategy for survival. He has learned that the human body is an organic whole, engaging all its parts in its functions. If one eats mechanically, without concentrating all one's senses on the meal, the body derives only partial benefit from the food. This is why, for Shukhov, eating becomes almost a sacrament and requires his total involvement. It is significant that at the evening meal Shukhov with his two bowls — his own and Caesar's — consolidates their contents so that he can concentrate fully on eating and need not guard the second bowl from theft.

Much of the food has already been stolen by the kitchen staff, composed of convicts, even before it is served. Thus Shukhov's thoughts about "these bastards in the kitchen"⁵ when he sees his neighbor's watery portion are entirely understandable. What is surprising is that Shukhov can feel some compassion for his fellow inmate and derives no satisfaction from comparing his own fairly good gruel (there is even one piece of potato in it) with his neighbor's. The most astonishing thought in Shukhov's mind is his optimistic hope for a favorable outcome to his desperate situation:

Shukhov didn't have a grudge in the world now — about how long his sentence was, about how long their day was, about that Sunday they wouldn't get. All he thought now was: "We'll get through! We'll get through it all! And God grant it'll all come to an end."⁶

Avoiding undesirable, distressing thoughts during his meals promotes the most complete digestion of his meager ration. Total immersion in eating is clearly part of his well-defined strategy for survival.

The fact that Shukhov regards his camp experience not exclusively as a completely unacceptable violation of normal human life, but also as an experience which can lead him to new, enriching perceptions, aids him in his struggle for survival. His re-evaluation of his former life lends him added strength for the psychological war he wages with the brutal camp authorities:

> In the camps he often remembered how they used to eat at home in the village — potatoes by the panful and pots of kasha, and in the early days before that, great hunks of meat. And they swilled enough milk to make their bellies burst. But he understood in the camps this was all wrong. You had to eat with all your thoughts on the food, like he was nibbling off these little bits now, and turn them over on your tongue, and roll them over in your mouth — and then it tasted so good, this soggy black bread. What had he eaten this eight years and more? Nothing at all. But the work he'd done on it![7]

Shukhov's re-evaluation is certainly not intended as a justification of the cruelty of the concentration camps. Solzhenitsyn obviously introduces the theme of food merely to demonstrate that, because of its very scarcity, the act of eating takes on new and profound importance for a prisoner such as Shukhov, who has the ability and the will to survive.

As the prisoners depend on daily work rates for their rations, the theme of labor is inevitably intertwined with that of food. The prisoners' work is badly organized, and the quotas are so high that even a completely healthy man could scarcely meet them in order to earn some extra bread. Furthermore, most of the prisoners labor under extremely harsh conditions. Their work is mainly construction in the open, where they are exposed to freezing winter temperatures. It is so cold that it is useless to carry a bucket of water to the construction site, for on the way the water would freeze into a chunk of solid ice. Instead the prisoners melt snow on a stove they have built inside a shelter at their work site for their own protection. With the utmost ingenuity and at some personal risk, they spend half a day contriving these elementary aids to their work and gathering firewood.

An understanding of the organization of a brigade — and the function of its boss, or foreman — is crucial to an appreciation of its role in the prisoners' struggle against death:

You might well ask why a prisoner worked so hard for ten years in a camp. Why didn't they say to hell with it and drag their feet all day long till the night, which was theirs?

But it wasn't so simple. That's why they'd dreamed up these [brigades]. It wasn't like [brigades] "outside," where every fellow got paid separately. In the camps they had these [brigades] to make the prisoners keep each other on their toes. So the fellows at the top didn't have to worry. It was like this — either you all got something extra or you all starved. ("You're not pulling your weight, you swine, and I've got to go hungry because of you. So work, you bastard!")[8]

Again it is a question of food, a question of survival under conditions of permanent starvation. The camp authorities and the foreman evaluate the work done collectively by the brigade, and distribute food accordingly. The work rating, a daily process in the camp, places almost superhuman power in the hands of the foreman. The quantity of food his brigade receives depends on his forcefulness and intelligence. The foreman must apply his ingenuity, not only to the negotiations with the camp authorities over work rates, but also to the work itself — he must organize his brigade in the most productive way to keep his men in shape for hard labor, for which food and warmth are essential. A single unfortunate day for a brigade may be critical. Poor working conditions are bound to affect its daily production negatively, and this decline in work in turn lowers the food ration. A day or two of reduced rations may start a general decline in the work of men already on their last legs, thus creating a vicious circle leading to the brigade's complete collapse. This is why the foreman has practically unlimited authority over his men:

That's how it was in your [brigade]. The higher-ups had a job to get a prisoner to work even in working hours, but your [foreman] only had to say the word, even if it was the meal break, and you worked. Because it was the [foreman] who fed you. And he wouldn't make you work if you didn't have to.[9]

The narrator elevates the brigade foreman almost to the status of a deity: "In a camp, your [brigade foreman] is everything. A good one can give you a new lease on life, but a bad one will finish you off."[10] The man on whom the existence of the entire brigade depends commands total loyalty, at least so far as Shukhov is concerned.

A good foreman who cares about his men struggles daily with the authorities for a higher evaluation of his brigade's work, for every operation must be rated according to official standards. The foreman has two methods of combatting the inhumanity of the camp bureaucracy. He can inflate the brigade's production if he is clever enough, or he can bribe the authorities to increase his men's rations. The currency he uses is, of course, food — either that received from the prisoners' families or extra rations.

The actual purpose of the brigade is thus not merely to organize workers. Rather it is a device through which the camp authorities squeeze the last bit of energy from each prisoner. Since the food is parcelled out, not individually, but to the entire brigade, every member looks after the others and everyone works as hard as possible, so that the prisoners in effect become their own guards:

> The foreman was like a rock. But he only had to raise an eyebrow or point a finger and you ran off to do what he wanted. You could cheat anyone you liked in the camp, but not Tyurin. That way you'd stay alive.[11]

In addition to starvation and exhaustion, the prisoners must endure the brutality of the camp authorities, the wardens and guards who subject them to constant terror and intimidation. The authorities have clearly defined roles: for all the senselessness of the rules and regulations, the prisoners at least know what to expect from their guards. The "prayer" which the commander of the guard traditionally recites before every march epitomizes the waste and absurd cruelty of Stalin's penal system:

> "Your attention, prisoners! You will keep strict column order on the line of march! You will not straggle or bunch up. You will not change places from one rank of five to another. You will not talk or look around to either side, and you will keep your arms behind you! A step to right or left will be considered an attempt at escape, and the escort will open fire *without* warning!"[12]

These rules were doubtless concocted in some central office of the Camps Administration to cover all possible situations, but many of the stipulations are ridiculously inapplicable to Shukhov's camp. There is no point in forbidding the prisoners to look around, for there is nothing to see on the way but bare steppe. It is equally senseless to forbid them to talk, since such a rule is unenforceable. The rules state that even one accidental step outside the column could cost a prisoner his life, but it would be pointless to open fire without warning, as no one could escape anyway on an open steppe from the escort equipped with automatic weapons and police dogs.

Drastic though this warning seems, it actually has little bearing on the prisoners' struggle for survival. The exhausting labor demanded of them, the systematic under-evaluation of their work which keeps them in permanent danger of starvation, and the arbitrary enforcement of certain rules have a far more deleterious effect on them. During the course of Shukhov's day, Lieutenant Volkovoy orders the removal of all extra clothing from the prisoners before they go to work in the bitter cold. This is unnecessarily cruel even by camp standards, and naturally provokes an emotional response from the convict Captain. The narrator mentions another instance in passing in his description of a rule which the administration could not fully enforce: an order to the prisoners never to appear outside the barracks alone, but always in groups of four or five. This rule is clearly impractical if not self-defeating, for the prisoners would all have to be jailed if it were enforced.

Ironically the prisoners actually suffer less from the oppression of the authorities than from the inequities imposed on them by their fellow inmates who enjoy a privileged position. Those prisoners who are assigned duties in managing the camp — running the kitchen, storing parcels, working in the camp hospital, supervising the brigades — actually collaborate with the authorities to perpetuate their power.

The greatest threat to the prisoners is the theft of their food by the kitchen staff. Eight convicts prepare lunch for the brigades. The cook — who could manage alone without much difficulty — does virtually nothing but pour the groats into a caldron and add some salt and any fat left over after all the cooks in the main kitchen have helped themselves to the supply. Nevertheless the cook's staff at the work-site kitchen consists of the following: one man to carry approximately twenty pounds of groats from the camp to the work site, one man to carry water, one to carry firewood, one to carry the bowls, one to guard the doors of the mess hall to prevent the bowls from being taken out, and another to collect them from all over the work site, for they are taken out anyway. Besides these six men, there is a sanitary inspector who does nothing but look on, and a brigade foreman who tests the food.

The Captain underscores the desperate situation of the prisoners

when he and Caesar discuss Eisenstein's film *Potemkin,* specifically
the scene in which the crew discovers worms in the rotten meat in
the ship's kitchen: "If they brought that kind of meat to the camp,
I can tell you, and put it in the caldron instead of that rotten fish we
get, I bet we'd . . ."[13] The hypocrisy of assigning a sanitary inspector to the kitchen staff in a camp where, as the Captain suggests,
the prisoners would be happy to eat wormy meat, is laughable. Yet
the thoughtful camp administration wants to be assured that the
prisoners' food meets not only high sanitary standards, but high
gastronomical standards as well. One wonders what would happen
if the sanitary inspector and the brigade foreman who serves as
taster were to decide one day to reject the meal. The prisoners
themselves would doubtless kill them, since there would be no
replacement for the rejected lunch.

In his exposé of the food service, Solzhenitsyn also ridicules the
pomposity of the cook, who acts like a French chef in a resort
hotel. His function is to boil some water with groats, a meal that
any Boy Scout could prepare over a campfire. The tremendous
authority the cook enjoys is based, not on his skill, but on his control of the food. His lordly manner is patently false, and his
extravagant corps of assistants for every single operation is
grotesque.

## II   *The Struggle Against the Camp System*

The narrator's description of the mess points to the general situation in Stalin's empire, or for that matter in any society living
according to a double standard. Theoretically, during Stalin's
regime one had the right to a fair trial, but Shukhov agreed to plead
guilty to the false accusation of espionage, since the alternative was
a firing squad. A prisoner had the right to receive food parcels
from his family, but the food supply all over the country was so
poor that Shukhov asked his wife not to send him any packages.
(Of course, there were some in the Soviet Union who could afford
to send food parcels to their imprisoned relatives. Caesar, for
example, receives parcels regularly but does not consume very
much of the food himself, as every man with any authority expects
a bribe from him.) Theoretically a prisoner had the right to send
letters home, but the censorship was so strict that nothing meaningful could be communicated. Theoretically a prisoner had the right
to complain, and there is a special box in Shukhov's camp for writ-

ten grievances, but no one ever checks it. Theoretically also, a prisoner was protected by law against abuse and cruel treatment; yet when the Captain, new to the camp, raises his voice during the morning search on the assumption that there is some kind of legal regulation of the treatment of prisoners in a labor camp, he discovers that practice and theory are light-years apart:

"You've no right to strip people in the cold! You don't know Article Nine of the Criminal Code!"
They had the right and they knew the article. You've still got a lot to learn, brother.
"You're not Soviet people," the Captain kept on at them. "You're not Communists!"
Volkovoy could take the stuff about the Criminal Code, but this made him mad. He looked black as a thundercloud and snapped at him:
"Ten days' solitary!"[14]

The narrator is right: there is nothing new the Captain could possibly say to Lieutenant Volkovoy, but the latter is well prepared to deal with such an upstart. Ten days in solitary, as we learn from the narrator at the end of the day, "meant you'd be a wreck for the rest of your life. You got TB and you'd never be out of hospitals long as you lived. And the fellows who did fifteen days were dead and buried."[15] A seemingly peaceful day thus turns into a confrontation with death. Every prisoner in the camp, as well as many people elsewhere in Stalin's empire, is constantly staring straight into the eyes of death.

### III　*Kuzyomin's Code*

Three mortal enemies constantly stalk a prisoner: starvation, exhaustion, and annihilation by the authorities. These three perils are particularly important in understanding Ivan Denisovich Shukhov. At reveille, when we first meet him, he is presented as the lowest possible specimen of the human race. Like a well-trained dog, he is clever and tricky, yet reliable and obedient. Shukhov perceives the outside world through sounds, as a dog or a cat would in his master's house on a quiet morning:

He didn't know why but nobody'd come to open up the barracks. And you couldn't hear the orderlies hoisting the latrine tank on the poles to carry it out.[16]

None of his thoughts or feelings is introverted. His mind and all his senses are concentrated on externals, almost exclusively on the most primitive features of his world. The first sentence of the novel containing Shukhov's name refers to one of the most basic bodily functions: "The sound stopped and it was pitch black on the other side of the window, just like in the middle of the night when Shukhov had to get up to go to the latrine. . . ."[17] Shukhov's usual activities (sweeping, mending, and so forth) during his ninety free minutes between reveille and breakfast are again of a very elementary nature. Moreover, they are servile and humiliating.

Up to this point Shukhov seems a man completely lacking in dignity and concerned with only one thought — how to get a better deal from his master and more food. Shukhov manifests his obsequiousness when the warden places him under camp arrest for failing to arise at reveille as a pretext for assigning him the duty of washing the floor in the warden's room:

"But what for, Comrade Warden?" Shukhov asked, and he made his voice sound more pitiful than he really felt. . . . But there wasn't a chance of getting out of it with the Tartar. So he went on asking to be let off just for the hell of it, but meantime pulled on his padded trousers.[18]

Shukhov knows very well that his humiliating plea for pardon is hopeless. It can be explained only as the desire of a completely suppressed man to demonstrate his loyalty to his merciless master, to please him through his own humiliation, and to provide his master with yet another opportunity to exercise his power and cruelty. This is the type of prisoner, and the kind of citizen, that the authorities preferred. It is doubtless easier to run a concentration camp populated by meek and broken pets or domestic animals than one with men like the Captain, who proclaim their rights and quote the criminal code.

Shukhov, however, is far from broken or reduced to the level of a pet, for there is another side to his character. The first sign of a dichotomy in his nature appears at the end of the passage enumerating all the services which he could perform during his free morning time. When he thinks of collecting the dirty bowls in the dining room, the narrator adds: "And the worst thing was that if there was something left in a bowl you started to lick it. You couldn't help it."[19] This is Shukhov's first introverted concern, his first acknowledgement of his own humanity. The temptation implies a kind of ethical standard of a man who tries to abide by his principles even in the most difficult of situations. The origin of his ethical code is described immediately:

And Shukhov could still hear the words of his first [brigade foreman], Kuzyomin — an old camp hand who'd already been inside for twelve years in 1943. Once, by a fire in a forest clearing, he'd said to a new batch of men just brought in from the front:
"It's the law of the jungle here, fellows. But even here you can live. The first to go is the guy who licks out bowls, puts his faith in the infirmary, or squeals to the screws."[20]

In 1943 Shukhov was in Camp Ust'-Izhma, where he almost died of diarrhea. Anyone aware of the conditions in a concentration camp can easily understand that when a prisoner becomes a so-called "goner," there is no hope for him unless help arrives either through food parcels from home or from some authority in the camp itself. The reader also knows that the brigade foreman is portrayed in this novel as a minor deity, empowered to give or take life. Shukhov's recalling Kuzyomin's words of 1943 hints that his bragade foreman may have saved Shukhov's life at that camp. The narrator's repeated mention of the spoon inscribed "Ust'-Izhma, 1944" which Shukhov cast himself, is further evidence of this. Apparently that year was crucial in Shukhov's life, a rebirth of sorts when his almost omnipotent brigade foreman, Kuzyomin, possibly imparted new life to him.

The first sentence of Kuzyomin's formula for survival literally reads, "Here, fellows, taiga is the law." The law of the taiga — a Russian word for virgin Siberian forest — is equivalent to the law of the beasts of the jungle — the struggle for sheer survival. "But people live even here," he continues, elaborating on the contrast between taiga and people. Thus the law of the taiga may be supplanted by the law of human culture and ethics. The last sentence reads: "Here are those who perish in a camp: those who lick bowls...." The plural form here clearly implies that the bowls belong to other prisoners. The remainder of the translation reflects the Russian original perfectlv.

Kuzyomin delivers his speech in a lonely clearing amidst the dark taiga, where a campfire is the only source of warmth and light. Around this fire sits a group of novices, ex-soldiers and ex-officers. The only experienced and knowledgeable man in this world of the taiga is Kuzyomin, who has already survived there for twelve years. The entire scene is permeated with the tone of a Biblical passage in which a prophet speaks to his people. Kuzyomin's code of life and death literally sounds like the word of God. One is in the hands of death here, Kuzyomin admits, but one can overcome its power, and live. He enumerates the three pitfalls to be avoided by those who want to win the confrontation with death, who want to survive: Do not lick other prisoners' bowls; do not depend on medical help; do not inform on one's fellow prisoners. Those who violate this code of conduct will die, for they will cease to be human beings.

The natural instinct of any human being struggling against starvation, exhaustion, and brutality would be to take any extra bit of nourishment, even from other prisoners' leftovers, to seek relief from enervating work by staying in the hospital for a day or two, and to remain on good terms with the camp authorities. Male prisoners, as Solzhenitsyn presents them, could achieve this third objective only by serving as informers. Kuzyomin emphatically rejects this seemingly safe strategy of survival in a labor camp. According to his observation, it is precisely those who follow their instincts who perish.

Kuzyomin's code is essential to the novel because it implicitly proclaims the primacy of spiritual values even in a struggle for physical survival. The code incorporates the paradox on which the entire Judeo-Christian ethic is based, i.e. that brute force is neither the source nor the guarantee of life. A man lives by sublimating his natural instincts, by experiencing the world spiritually. Without any reference to God, the Bible, or Christ, in a society which has for three decades suppressed all religious teaching, in the taiga by a lonely campfire at night, the essence of religion finds a new, precise formulation clear to anyone and requiring neither religious instruction nor cultural conditioning.

A peculiar feature of this spiritual message (if one may call it that) is that it promises nothing above and beyond the natural limits of human life. It does not deal with transcendental reality, for both the act and the result are practically within one's reach. There is neither salvation nor punishment in the hereafter; there is only the present struggle against one's annihilation. Life is its own reward.

Solzhenitsyn presumably slipped Kuzyomin's formula past the Soviet censors by omitting all religious references from it. Furthermore, Shukhov and the narrator seemingly refute the code, at least in part: "About the secret spying he, of course, exaggerated. Exactly those do survive. But their survival is paid by others' blood."[21] This critical comment *de facto* supports the general principal of Kuzyomin's formula — the primacy of spiritual values in the struggle against one's own annihilation. It is really not so important whether the informers survive or not. The important fact remains that, even while partially refuting Kyzyomin's code, the narrator adheres to his ethical standards and considers the blood of the fellow prisoners an unacceptable price to pay for survival.

The subject of informers arises again in the prisoners' discussion around a fire that prompts a flashback about Shukhov's experience in Camp Ust'-Izhma:

He stared into the fire and remembered his seven years in the North. . . . The Commandant's rule was — any brigade that didn't do its quota in the daytime was kept on the job at night. They used to get back to camp after midnight and go out again in the morning.
"Don't kid yourself, fellows, it's easier here," he said in his funny way. . . .
"The hell it's easier!" Fetyukov hissed. . . . "They slit your throat here while you're in bed! You call that easy?"
"That happens only to squealers, not human beings!" Pavlo put a finger up, like he was warning Fetyukov.[22]

The interrelationship of these two passages is clear. In addition to the similarity of the two settings, the focus is again on the struggle of man against the jungle, and again the brigade leader pronounces moral judgment. Pavlo, the assistant foreman, makes the final statement with a gesture of authority, clearly distinguishing, as Kuzyomin had, between those who survive and those who lose their human dignity and therefore perish.

The application of Kuzyomin's code by Ivan Denisovich on a particular day is the central theme of the novel. It is reflected in Shukhov's struggle for dignity and self-respect against the powers which would dehumanize and humiliate him to such an extent that his resistance and vitality break down. At this point he would become a vulnerable subject, precisely the type that his personality mirrors in the beginning of the novel.

Even during the morning march to the work site, it is apparent that Shukhov adheres faithfully to Kuzyomin's code. Reflecting on his family and the changes in his village during his absence, Shukhov speculates about the new, high earnings in the "carpet painting" trade. His inner conflict here is the same as the one he experiences when he has the opportunity to collect the dirty bowls in the dining room. Both the bowls with their leftovers and the carpet-painting business promise practical advantages, but both require the betrayal of one's own principles. Once a person has lost his moral compass and betrayed his own nature, he cannot enjoy any material rewards, for his life is already destroyed. Shukhov decides he will take to the carpet-painting business only as a last resort — if he becomes an outcast after his release from the concentration camp. If no other work is available, if the power structure denies him the possibility of earning an honest living, then — he thinks — he would have to compromise his moral code. These are all speculations about the future, however. While he is in prison, Shukhov does not compromise.

Along with his resisting the temptation to lick the bowls goes Shukhov's assumption of paternal responsibility in the only way possible under the circumstances: he refrains from asking his family to send him food parcels. Even while dying of starvation in Ust'-Izhma, he did not ask for food, since he knew that every ounce sent to him would mean that much less for his daughters. Shukhov possesses a miraculous abundance of spiritual strength, a capacity for love. In contrast to the average prisoner confronting death in a concentration camp, where there is no room for sentiment, Shukhov appears noble:

> Gopchik brought along some new aluminum wire, the kind electricians used.
> He said: "Ivan Denisovich! This is good wire for spoons. Will you teach me how to make a spoon?"
> Ivan Denisovich liked this little rascal Gopchik (his own son had died young, and he had two grown-up daughters at home)....
> They broke off some wire to make spoons and hid it in a corner.[23]

Shukhov more or less adopts Gopchik, and teaches him the skills needed for survival in the camp. The Russian verb for "liked" which the narrator uses to describe Ivan Denisovich's affection for Gopchik could be translated as "loved," and indeed the text seems to point toward the more profound feeling. Although Shukhov is ill (he even sought admission to the hospital this morning) and lacks the energy or time for extra work, he hides a piece of wire in order to show Gopchik how to cast a spoon later. This child is personally important to Shukhov, as his own son would be. Through

Gopchik, Shukhov expresses his paternal feelings actively, just as he expresses them *in absentia* by refusing to deprive his family of food.

Though he is well aware that Gopchik is receiving packages, and even knows when the boy is secretly eating his food, Shukhov does not expect anything from his "adopted son," just as he does not deprive his children at home of anything. Gopchik obviously could afford to pay him in the same way the other prisoners do for his various services — with food — but Shukhov makes an exception for Gopchik, takes nothing from him, and — the narrator implies — even rationalizes the boy's selfishness by commenting, "You couldn't feed everyone anyway."[24] Gopchik is doubtless very special to Shukhov. Their relationship parallels the role Kuzyomin apparently played in Shukhov's life during his first years in prison.

Fetyukov is the antithesis of Kuzyomin's ideal: he is a man who does not resist the law of the taiga, and is therefore doomed. Fetyukov's perception of life and his behavior are reminiscent of Shukhov as we glimpse him initially. Later, however, from behind the mask Shukhov dons as the perfect prisoner, or slave, there emerges a free man struggling to preserve his honor and dignity. Fetyukov, on the contrary, is totally broken.

In the prisoners' relationship with the authorities, the Captain represents the other extreme. By openly opposing the authorities, he violates the spirit of Kuzyomin's code, which — by omitting any reference to the assertion of one's ego — implies that a prisoner should refrain from active protest or from distinguishing himself from the grey mass of convicts. As any experienced prisoner knows, open resistance is totally senseless. The problems that the inmates in Stalin's concentration camps face are too serious to sacrifice oneself for a momentary victory or the temporary satisfaction of letting off steam. A prisoner has to survive from ten to twenty-five years: this is his main assignment.

Shukhov is a blend of all three types of prisoner: Kuzyomin's pupil, Fetyukov (the facade Shukhov shows to the authorities but tries to suppress in himself), and the Captain (the side Shukhov reveals when Tyurin, Klevshin, and Pavlo threaten to attack the supervisor, Der). Clearly, Shukhov too is ready to defend his fellow prisoners' lives, even at the risk of violence.

The most dramatic presentation of the two Shukhovs — the slave and the free man — occurs during the evening, when he sees Caesar surveying the contents of his parcel:

> Caesar was already sitting in his lower bunk and gaping at the stuff. He'd spread it all out on his bed and on the locker, but it was a little dark because the light from the bulb on the ceiling was cut off by Shukhov's bunk. Shukhov bent down, got between the Captain's bunk and Caesar's, and handed over the bread ration. "Your bread, Caesar Markovich."
>
> He didn't say, "So you got it," because this would've been hinting about how he stood in line for him and that he had a right to a cut. He knew he had, but even after eight years of hard labor he was still no scavenger and the more time went on, the more he stuck to his guns.[25]

The last phrase is crucial to an understanding of the text. A more literal translation reads as follows: "But he was not a jackal even after eight years in the camps, and the more time went on, the firmer he became about this."

The word Solzhenitsyn uses here for "firm" is an obsolete term, often found in religious texts describing saints who grew ever stronger in their faith and asceticism by overcoming temptations. This barely noticeable, phraseological indicator points ultimately to the paradox implicit in Kuzyomin's code. The man who chooses not to yield to the pressure of the taiga will slowly discover a source of spiritual strength and — instead of growing weaker, as one might expect — will reaffirm his devotion to his principles and become unshakable in his determination. Without this final illustration of Kuzyomin's code, Shukhov would inevitably become another Fetyukov, and that part of Shukhov which resembles a tame animal or a slave would subsume his entire being. Time, however, begins to work not against but for the man who lives in accordance with Kuzyomin's precepts. Shukhov's spiritual strength does not erode but increases, and the more he sacrifices for the sake of his inner freedom and dignitys, the more strength he acquires for future confrontations with death.

Solzhenitsyn's novel is, however, not a hagiographic text. Shukhov is not an icon, an idealized image. Like every human being, he is both strong and weak:

> But he wasn't master of his eyes. Like all the others he had the eyes of a hawk, and in a flash they ran over the things Caesar had laid out on the bed and the locker. But though he still hadn't taken the paper off them or opened the bags, Shukhov couldn't help telling by this quick look — and a sniff of the nose — that Caesar had gotten sausage, canned milk, a large smoked fish, fatback, crackers with one kind of smell and cookies with another, and about four pounds of lump sugar. And then there was butter, cigarettes, and pipe tobacco. And that wasn't the end of it.

Shukhov saw all this in the time it took him to say "Your bread, Caesar Markovich."[26]

This is the Shukhov we encounter at the very beginning of the novel. As earlier he listened, now he sniffs, and with the same precision as before he recognizes the "crackers with one kind of smell and cookies with another." The introduction of these symptoms of adaptation to the taiga is not accidental. The development of those instincts usually associated with animals is inevitable in human beings who are treated like beasts. Solzhenitsyn's hero manages to adapt himself to brutish conditions while remaining human in the noblest sense of the word.

Shukhov learns the precepts by which he lives from Kuzyomin and, in turn, passes them on to Gopchik, his "adopted son," by personal example. Though Shukhov cannot articulate the principle, he lives by it more than adequately.

In January, 1951, Shukhov has almost completed his sentence. He may receive an additional ten years, or he may be released. As the reader sees him during one day of his life, he has still not compromised and shows no inclination to abandon the struggle for both moral and physical survival. Thus one may assume that, should he receive a second ten-year term, he has a good chance of surviving even that, and eventually regaining his freedom.

### IV   *Varieties of Spiritual Resistance*

Prisoner Y-81 provides an example of such extended resistance. One sees him only from a distance, as one would view an icon in a church. Shukhov notices him in the dining hall, thinks about him briefly, and although he does not make any comment, one may be certain that the image of this man who gives not one inch in his struggle against the law of the taiga and the formidable power of Stalin's empire remains stored somewhere in Shukhov's memory.

The description of Y-81 recalls the asceticism of Byzantine iconography. His appearance is stern; his expression, meditative or praying; his face, worn and seemingly chiseled from stone. The authorities' systematic addition of ten-year terms to his sentence coupled with his firm resolve never to give in drives him to martyrdom. Y-81 refuses to compromise in his attempt to preserve dignity and beauty in his life. Sitting up straight, he places his bread on a clean cloth and lifts his wooden spoon — his symbolic link with ancient

Russian tradition — high to his mouth.

Shukhov also exhibits great resolution, but is much more worldly than Y-81. Shukhov is actively engaged in the struggle for survival; he steals extra portions; his eyes are everywhere; he notices everything. Both men express the spirit of Kuzyomin's code. Both maintain their dignity, try to preserve at least minimal esthetic appearances, and manage to preserve what is noble in their spirits while barely surviving under the law of the taiga. Shukhov, however, is not an iconographic image but rather the mundane mirror of the ideal Y-81 represents. Shukhov loves Gopchik, has compassion for others (even Fetyukov), and shares his bit of extra food with Alyoshka the Baptist:

> "Here, Alyoshka." Shukhov gave him one of the cookies.
> Alyoshka smiled. "Thank you, but you haven't got very much yourself."
> "Go ahead. Eat it." It was true he didn't have very much but *he* could always earn something.[27]

In this act of magnanimity and genuine love, Kuzyomin-Shukov's and Alyoshka's philosophies merge. Alyoshka, a believer in the mystical power of prayer taught by the Church, asks Shukhov to pray to God, for prayer is Alyoshka's only source of inner strength. Although Shukhov as a rule does not pray, he has tremendous moral strength which does not erode under the pressure of time and circumstance. Thus, in terms of man's mystical relationship with God, Shukhov's and Alyoshka's philosophies coincide again, and Kuzyomin's code becomes a creed for the concentration camp.

Shukhov's sigh, "Thanks to Thee, O Lord, one more day has passed,"[28] is not necessarily an expression of religious devotion but rather a folk phrase that even an irreligious person might utter. Alyoshka takes it literally, however, and seizes upon it to launch an attempt to convert Shukhov to Christianity. Alyoshka fails in his mission, partly because the religious terminology in which he couches his sermon is inappropriate to life in a concentration camp, hardly the proper context for evangelical metaphors. It is superfluous to speak of moving mountains to a man whose very survival under the conditions described in this novel is already a mirccle in itself. Shukhov poignantly demonstrates the point by translating Alyoshka's reference to daily bread from the Lord's Prayer into the

language of the *zeks:* "You mean that ration we get?"[29] It is difficult to find more precise parallel to the evangelical concept of daily
bread than the daily, 100-gram bread ration in a labor camp.
Shukhov does not really need to be converted. With his faultless
sense of life, he formulates precisely the point which Alyoshka has
failed to make:

"Look, Alyoshka," Shukhov said, "it's all right for you. It was Christ
told you to come here, and you are here because of Him. But why am *I*
here? Because they didn't get ready for the war like they should've in
forty-one? Was that *my* fault?"[30]

The problem here lies in the juxtaposition of meaningful and
senseless suffering — imprisonment that leads to spiritual growth
on the one hand, and that which leads only to physical and spiritual
decay, as in the case of Fetyukov. Nothing is more absurd and in its
way grotesque than a man's serving ten or twenty-five years in one
of Stalin's concentration camps because Stalin himself failed to
prepare the USSR for the war. Seen in this light, Shukhov's senseless suffering in the camp ought to be unbearable; yet his day as
described in the novel demonstrates exactly the opposite. Shukhov
and Alyoshka's conversation at the end of the day is structurally
related to Kuzyomin's speech introduced as a flashback at the
beginning of the novel. These two passages, which contrast with the
general setting, are as unexpected as the image of Y-81, who rises
majestically above the grey, depersonalized mass of prisoners eating in the dining hall.

Kuzyomin's precepts, insofar as they reflect the Judeo-Christian
spiritual tradition, assure survival for any prisoner who maintains
his human dignity and spiritual standards under the law of the
taiga. This code is valid for all prisoners threatened with destruction and death — believers as well as atheists — and gives them a
sense of life and the means to struggle for it. In the kingdom of
death, in one of Stalin's prison camps, it means nothing to speak of
reward and punishment in a direct, simplistic way. It is likewise
absurd to speak of the Last Judgment, for surely that is here and
now. Those prisoners who remain human remain alive; those who
lose their humanity perish.

Solzhenitsyn relies heavily on the anonymous narrator-
commentator to convey the theme of spiritual resistance and struggle. The fact that the narrator's language resembles Shukhov's and

that the narrative has the quality of an oral account makes this novel especially difficult to translate, since it is virtually impossible to render many of its important nuances in another language. In the Russian text, for example, Big Ivan, one of the guards, is described with the archaic poetic (or religious) epithet, *chernookii,* meaning "black-eyed." In context the word possesses a spiritual nuance not reflected in the English translation, for the sergeant stands in personal opposition to the camp authoriites and Stalin's entire system of oppression. Big Ivan's benevolence towards the prisoners entails no small risk and could easily convert his position from that of guard to guarded.

The narrator's style is crucial to an interpretation of the novel. The entire two hundred pages are written without any chapter divisions, as the narrator seemingly tells his story in a single breath, without pauses, extemporaneously. The very spontaneity of the narrative is intrinsic to the novel; it is a technique designed to create the impression of a completely sincere and truthful account of circumstances, people, their lives, their struggles against death, and their heroism under conditions which would normally defy belief.

In addition to the credibility the narrator lends to the description of events, he provides concrete details for appreciating the significance and function of Kuzyomin's code in the novel. Only a man who is both a veteran prisoner and who fully comprehends Kuzyomin's precepts could elucidate Shukhov's true character, so carefully concealed both from the authorities and from the majority of his fellow prisoners. In the passage describing his exuberance at slipping a small piece of metal past the guards, the narrator demonstrates his insight into Shukhov's practical, realistic spirituality which is perfectly attuned to the rigors of camp life. While the guard is searching him, Shukhov prays fervently to God to save him. Then, elated over his narrow escape, he runs "to catch up with the others. . . . He felt like he was walking on air but he didn't say a prayer of thanks because there wasn't any time and there was no sense in it now."[31]

One may suspect a certain cynicism in this last comment, if it is taken out of context; but for Shukhov, who lives according to the principles of Kuzyomin's code, an expression of gratitude would be an unnecessary formality. In the view of the narrator as well as Shukhov, the original prayer to God from the total darkness of the kingdom of the taiga itself amounts to a profession of faith and gratitude for His help.

Kuzyomin's code extends beyond the concrete situation in which it arose to embrace the entire human experience. The three precepts indicate that the most essential values for survival are spiritual, and that betrayal of these values is suicidal. Kuzyomin's commandments contain the concept of preserving one's freedom even in a concentration camp, that modern institution of slavery. The prisoners' total subjection to the law of the taiga compels them to submit to the brutal suppression of the camp administration. The only defense against the destructive will of the authorities is the preservation of one's own humanity. This is the sole means of retaining one's self-respect and, consequently, preserving any meaning and purpose in life. Ultimately, Kuzyomin's code leads to victory over death in the concentration camp — and, by extension, elsewhere as well.

CHAPTER 3

# The Cancer Ward

### I  *The Setting of the Novel*

SOLZHENITSYN'S second novel, *The Cancer Ward,* ostensibly deals with the lives of doctors and patients in a hospital. The first few chapters bear a strong resemblance to the archetypal medical story; indeed, on at least one level the events leading up to the second half of the book may be read in this light. As the plot develops, however, one comes to question how central a role the hospital, disease, and medical procedures actually play in the novel, whether it is not something else, having little in common with medicine *per se,* that constitutes the main theme. That theme is the duality of life, the discrepancy between the illusion of health and the terrifying reality of disease and death, both of individuals and of an entire society.

The plot is simple. Two cancer patients arrive almost at the same time at a hospital in Tashkent. Pavel Rusanov, a Party member, is an exponent of the power structure, while Oleg Kostoglotov, an ex-convict, represents the underprivileged stratum of Soviet society. Ironically, these two characters find themselves in the same ward in adjacent beds. Kostoglotov falls in love with a young woman doctor, Vera Gangart, and also flirts with a medical student who is working in the hospital as a nurse. The latter warns Kostoglotov about the side effects of the hormone therapy which he is undergoing. In his discussions with the doctors and ideological clashes with his fellow patients, Kostoglotov questions basic human values and the authority of medicine and the state to shape lives. Both of Kostoglotov's forays into love are abortive. He leaves the hospital only half cured, and the novel ends with him en route to his place of exile. His political antagonist, Rusanov, also leaves the hospital uncured.

48

The novel opens with the arrival of Rusanov at a cancer ward. The personnel director of a large industrial enterprise in Tashkent, one of the most important cities in the Asiatic USSR, he controls, constantly updates, and extends the personal files on all the employees. Because his work requires close collaboration with the omnipotent MGB (the secret police), Rusanov enjoys great authority both professionally and socially. Needless to say, he is a member of the Communist Party, or of the upper class. Consequently he expects special treatment, which his wife demands on his behalf from the moment he arrives at the hospital.

Near the end of the novel the scene in which Rusanov's wife and younger children come to take him home is one of overwhelming joy, for he is presumably cured of cancer. The children's vacation has just begun; Rusanov's son has passed his driver's examination and proudly drives the family home in their new automobile; the two older children are secure and happy. One of Rusanov's sons is a lawyer; although he causes his father considerable worry, Rusanov is still proud of him and his position. The older daughter is a promising young journalist and poet. What Rusanov does not realize as he joyfully leaves the hospital is that the prognosis for his disease is poor. He is departing only temporarily, for his malignant tumor has not been arrested.

The narrator immediately establishes the contrast between Rusanov and the protagonist of the novel, Oleg Kostoglotov, and the unfolding of the narrative only deepens the gulf between them. In contrast to Rusanov's ceremonial admission to the hospital, Kostoglotov arrives alone, wearing remnants of an old army uniform and carrying a dirty military knapsack. It is a rainy January evening, and his clothes are quite drenched. The treatment of his tumor is long overdue, and he is obviously suffering severe pain. Kostoglotov's papers are in order, but as he has arrived from a very remote and small settlement, he has been unable to make reservations in the hospital. On the evening of his arrival there is not a single empty bed. When a nurse informs him that he must spend the night elsewhere, Kostoglotov simply plops down on the floor and announces that he will not budge until the hospital admits him.

Unlike Rusanov, Kostoglotov belongs to that segment of society which is deprived of its rights and is condemned to its desperate situation forever. An ex-convict, he is not allowed to return to his native city of Leningrad. Instead, he is sent to a settlement selected by the authorities, where he must stay the rest of his life. This is why his treatment has been so delayed. For months the authorities at his settlement refused to allow him to travel as far as Tashkent for treatment. As exiles may not stay in hotels, Kostoglotov has no place to spend the night.

One may see just from these few observations that *The Cancer Ward* is much more than a medical story. None of the social, political, and philosophical contrasts and contradictions which Solzhenitsyn introduces in this novel is characteristic of the typical hospital story. He seems to have chosen a hospital as the setting of his novel for other reasons. Passages dealing with medicine form an important part of the book, but here again he employs medical terminology metaphorically, for the most part, to convey his message. One must remember that the action takes place in a cancer ward, and that all of the patients and doctors are confronting a potentially fatal disease. Every character in the novel — except perhaps some minor ones such as Nelly, a young orderly — is preoccupied with death. The fear of death and the horrible suffering of the dying pervade the novel. In this context, human relations become simpler, more open and honest. Men facing their own death through the slow progress of a disease and confined to the rigid routine of a hospital, where there is little distraction, are inevitably forced to reexamine their own past and ask themselves in one form or another those questions about the meaning of life rarely explored so intensively by physically healthy men. These essential questions form one of the major themes of the novel, and evidently prompted Solzhenitsyn to set it in a cancer ward.

The constant presence of cancer and inevitable death emphasizes the crucial role of the doctor, making him the almost complete master of the fate of others. The authority of the doctor over his patients' daily lives, and often their futures as well, raises the question of a human being's right to set his own standards, to determine independently the quality and length of his life rather than to accept passively the decisions reached by scientific and social institutions.

Finally, the constant struggle with incurable disease raises the problem of the reliability of knowledge — in this case, medical knowledge. The problem is whether the often deadly medical practices employed in the struggle against fatal diseases are justified, whether the treatment serves its supposed ends or instead merely deceives the patient.

The range of problems posed in *The Cancer Ward* is broad. The eternal, universal concepts of life and death are projected onto the background of twentieth-century civilization, with its scientific progress and social institutions. Solzhenitsyn associates modern medical care with politics in terms of the benefits both offer and the suffering they engender. The clash between an individual patient (Kostoglotov) and the entire medical establishment of a country is paralleled by the confrontation between certain characters in the novel and the political system. Just as every patient in the cancer ward lives under the shadow of a fatal disease, so does every man in one way or another live under the shadow of the gigantic police system of the totalitarian state. Some characters administer the system, while others are subjected to it. According to official doctrine, all should benefit from it. In Solzhenitsyn's view, society is totally controlled by two principal powers: science, the major instrument of industrial progress; and the state, the major instrument of political purpose. Both powers are essentially hostile to humanity. The key to this novel lies in the interaction of these primary themes. With this in mind, one should not be at all surprised to discover that social and political conflicts as well as philosophical problems constitute the theme of this novel.

The action is for the most part restricted to one ward in a large hospital. A total of thirteen patients — many of whom are subsequently released because their cases are incurable — occupy the nine beds in the room at one time or another. Closest to the door is Dyomka, a teenage trade school student with cancer of the leg. When his leg is later amputated, Shulubin occupies his bed. A Party member since 1917, Shulubin embarked upon a brilliant academic career in his youth, but during and after Stalin's purges his position was gradually reduced to that of librarian in a provincial agricultural college. In the next two beds are a Kazakh and an Uzbek, each speaking only his mother tongue. Chaly, a representative of the new class of black marketeers, later occupies the second bed from Dyomka. Second from the window is Rusanov, the Party member. Next to him and the window is Kostoglotov, who stands at the opposite end of the social spectrum.

On the other side of the room, opposite Kostoglotov, is Azovkin, who is eventually sent home to die. Vadim Zatsyrko, a brilliant, young geologist, a staunch Marxist, and a Party member, comes to occupy the bed. Next to Vadim is Yefrem Podduyev, a primitive man of brutal strength. In the past he has worked in many capacities, including supervising convict laborers. Released with incurable cancer of the tongue, he dies in the Tashkent railroad station on his way home. Federau, a Party member exiled because of his German ancestry, occupies Podduyev's vacated bed, and later the one on Rusanov's left. (Thus Rusanov, the proper Party member, finds himself sandwiched between two exiles — Kostoglotov on the one side and Federau on the other). Next to Podduyev is Akhmadzhan an Uzbek in the armed services and the only Asiatic patient in the room who speaks Russian. Later the reader learns that Akhmadzhan has been a concentration camp guard somewhere in Siberia. Next to the door is Proshka's bed. Sibgatov, a Crimean Tatar, one of the most touching characters in the novel, is placed in the corridor. He is testimony to one of Stalin's cruelest crimes, the deportation of the entire Crimean Tatar people from their native region.

This thirteenth ward is the center of the action in the novel. Occasionally, however, the reader glimpses other parts of the hospital and some of the patients in them. A professor of philosophy ironically suffering from cancer of the throat wanders over from the surgical wing now and then, and Dyomka visits Aunt Stefa, an old religious Russian woman with a large and loving family, who shares her food and Christian beliefs with him.

The fact that no one actually dies in the ward makes this disease, which springs from nowhere and drags its victims off to perish out of sight, seem even more sinister. The reader witnesses only part of its deadly course: the initial despair of the newcomer to the ward, his pain, his treatment, his waxing hopes, then the slow decline in the efficacy of the treatment, new and worse suffering, and finally the patient's release without any assurance of future health or even life.

The inhuman conditions under which the patients live reinforce the meaninglessness of this suffering, which indiscriminately invades human lives. None of the patients except Kostoglotov knows the nature of his treatment, its side effects, or the risks it involves. Without this knowledge, they lack the ability to decide on the most basic questions affecting their lives and become the completely dehumanized objects of another's will. The physicians have the best of intentions but are ineffectual and, furthermore, cannot alter the prevailing attitudes in the hospital toward the care of the sick. Thus the doctors are no freer than their patients. Though the physicians have the most idealistic aspirations, they inevitably succumb to the accepted medical dogmas, which undergo harsh criticism in this novel.

The two most important doctors are Lyudmila Dontsova, the chief radiologist, and her assistant, Vera Gangart. Both women are devoted physicians and fine specialists. Doctor Dontsova, a woman of unusual ability and willpower, is finally broken when she contracts cancer herself and is forced to seek treatment in Moscow. Doctor Gangart in a way undermines her own authority by deviating from one of the most fundamental rules of the hospital and allowing herself to enter into a personal relationship with her patient Kostoglotov.

Only conversations, reading, and the rounds of the doctors break the monotonous hospital routine. The ideological tension of the book originates in all three of these distractions. The attraction between the two teenagers Dyomka and Asya, and the romantic triangle among Kostoglotov, Zoya, and Vega which seemingly constitute the plot are in fact only peripheral to it. The action consists of ideological clashes among patients and between patient and doctor. The striking differences in the patients' social status and the constant fear of death reinforce the tension. These conflicts provide the focus of this analysis.

## II  *A Dialogue of Philosophies*

Solzhenitsyn employs the patients' conversations in large part in order to introduce various philosophies which conflict with one another, as nearly every character in the novel briefly formulates his *Weltanschauung*. This technique, quite characteristic of Solzhenitsyn, is most effectively employed in *The Cancer Ward*. The patients begin to articulate their individual philosophies after the barely literate Podduyev reads Tolstoy's short story "What Men Live By." Slowly, almost syllable by syllable, Podduyev reads the story that Tolstoy composed exactly for people like Podduyev, those barely touched by Western civilization. Podduyev realizes that his cancer is incurable, and his fear of death colors his perception of the story. Profoundly moved by its simplicity and sensitivity, he is eager to share the extraordinary experience of reading it. Naively he poses to his roommates the question that the story raises: "What do men live by?"

Akhmadzhan is the first to respond. He reacts as would a man about to be released from the hospital after successful treatment. He is a tragic figure who has been plucked from his native land, with its ancient and sophisticated culture, and transplanted by a depersonalized institution such as the army — or, as the reader later discovers the MGB — into a foreign milieu. Consequently, the most primitive concepts and attitudes have replaced the traditional wisdom of his nation in his mind. He answers the question "What do men live by?" with the mentality and the jargon of a soldier, replying "confidently and happily, because he was getting better, 'Their rations. Uniforms and supplies.'"[1]

With amazing naïveté, Podduyev continues to seek an answer. The theme of the degradation of human beings through the loss of national roots recurs in the implied comparison between the old Uzbek Mursalimov, and the young Karakalpak medical student Turgun. Mursalimov is totally unaffected by foreign culture. He does not even speak Russian, but it is apparent that his answer to Podduyev's question would enlighten the other patients if the language barrier did not prevent him from responding. Turgun, on the other hand, approaches Western civilization on a high scientific level; but, being spiritually alienated from his native land, he reverts to primitivism. His answer to the question is on the same gross level as Akhmadzhan's, though expressed in different words: "By their pay, that's what."[2]

Sibgatov, the Crimean Tatar, a member of one of the minority nations which Stalin brutally uprooted and relocated in various parts of Siberia completely alien to them, in answering the question offers a mild reproach to Akhmadzhan and Turgun, who obviously do not treasure their national heritage:

> Sibgatov sighed and said shyly, "Your homeland."
> "What's that?" asked Yefrem in surprise.
> "You know, the place you were born in ... living in the place you were born."[3]

Even Sibgatov's only slightly higher standard is too much for Podduyev, who has lived according to Dyomka's schoolboy definition of the essence of life, namely food and the satisfaction of one's basic physical needs:

> "Yes ... in my opinion," Dyomka announced slowly, as if answering a teacher at the blackboard, trying not to make a mistake, and still thinking it out between the words, "...In the first place, air. Then — water. Then — food."[4]

Podduyev adds to that only vodka. Professional skill, which

Proshka suggests as the essential ingredient, could provide the alcohol. The discussion remains on the same elementary, materialistic level on which Akhmadzhan had placed it.

The next day Dyomka, faced with the amputation of his leg, seeks someone to talk to and meets an attractive girl, Asya, who is also seeking company. Their conversation naturally turns to life in the hospital and the recent discussion in Dyomka's ward of Tolstoy's question:

> "Pah!" Asya had an answer for everything. "We had an essay about that at school: 'What does man live for?' They gave us study material full of cotton growers, milkmaids, Civil War heroes. 'What is your attitude to the brave deed of Pavel Korchagin?' 'What is your attitude to the heroism of Matrosov?'"
>
> "What *is* your attitude?"
>
> "Well what? Should we do what they did? The teachers said we should. So we all wrote that we would. Why spoil things just before the exams? But Sashka Gromov said, 'Do I have to write all that? Can't I write what I really think?' Our teacher said, 'I'll give you what you really think. You'll get the worst mark you've ever known.'...."[5]

The indoctrination in the schools is apparently so simplistic that only the most uncritical minds can take it seriously. The children are left to search alone for values to make their lives meaningful. Asya's answer to Tolstoy's question reveals the cynicism of her generation, alienated as it is from the ideals of its parents:

> "What for? What do you mean? For love, of course."
>
> For love! Tolstoy had said "For love" too, but in what sense? And the girl's teacher had made them write "For love" too, but in what sense? After all, Dyomka was used to having things precise in his mind, to working them out for himself.
>
> "But ..." he began hoarsely. (It was simple enough, perhaps, but rather embarrassing to say.) "After all, love is ... love isn't the whole of your life. It only happens ... sometimes. From a certain age, and up to a certain age...."
>
> "What age? From what age?" Asya interrogated him angrily as though he had offended her. "It's best at our age. When else? What is there in life except love?"[6]

Asya concludes her account of prostitution and pregnancy among the teenagers in her school with the exhortation: "The earlier you start, the more exciting it is.... Why wait? It's the atomic age!"[7]

Meanwhile the debate in the men's ward turns political. Rusanov's response sounds as if it stemmed from the primitive indoctrination in Asya's high school:

"Remember: people live by their ideological principles and by the interests of their society." . . .
Yefrem did not answer. He was annoyed that this pipsqueak had managed to wriggle out of it so cleverly. When it came to ideology, it was better to keep your trap shut.[8]

Intimidated, Podduyev fails to realize that Tolstoy's story is independent of party ideology. There remains a question about the second part of Rusanov's answer, "the interests of their society," however. At this point a confusion of terms arises. Rusanov's viewpoint — that of a member of the power structure — is vastly different from that of such a primitive man as Podduyev. The latter conceives of the interests of society as something similar to love, or at the very least as a sort of charity toward others:

Somehow they both tied up.
"What do they live by?" He could not say it aloud somehow. It seemed almost indecent. "It says here, by love."[9]

This is the first time in the novel that Tolstoy's fundamental spiritual concept is articulated, and it instantly reverses the roles of Rusanov and Podduyev. Now it is Rusanov who shows his profound naïveté, born not of simplicity but of arrogance. A man such as he, engaged in secret surveillance, could never identify that official propagandistic cliché "the interests of society" with love: "*Love?*. . . No, that's nothing to do with our sort of morality."[10] Rusanov's merciless self-characterization is devastating. Having rejected love, in accordance with the official ethic of his totalitarian government, he immediately follows his professional instincts and begins to investigate the source of this heretical teaching. Maybe the author should be investigated; maybe his files should be reexamined. "Listen, who wrote all that, anyway?" he demands to know.[11] But Tolstoy is out of Rusanov's reach.

In the evening after Dyomka's conversation with Asya, he returns to his ward, where a lively discussion is underway. Kostoglotov is describing a miraculous new cure for cancer. During his chaotic speech he quotes from a medical textbook in which the

authors present a few rare cases of self-induced cures and admit
that the relationship between malignant tumors and the central nervous system still remains a mystery. One can imagine how this news
is received in a cancer ward by nine patients clutching at every straw
of hope for survival. Kostoglotov, who missed the previous discussion provoked by Podduyev's question, is unaware of the spiritual
change that the latter has undergone after reading Tolstoy's story.
Spiritual enlightenment sometimes occurs suddenly, however, and
Podduyev's horizons have broadened considerably during the last
few hours. Now he breaks the silence in the ward by remarking
pessimistically:

"I suppose for that you need to have ... a clear conscience.... I've
mucked so many women about, left them with children hanging round
their necks. They cried ... mine'll never resolve."[12]

Rusanov's reaction to Podduyev's repentance is two-fold. Ini-
tially Rusanov could not tolerate Podduyev's pessimistic candor.
What Rusanov now objects to is not Podduyev's rude and tactless
manner, but his new ethical perspective, his rapid adoption of
Christian ethics in the Tolstoyan variant. Rusanov can tolerate
Podduyev neither as a primitive materialist nor as a new convert to
Christianity:

"What's [conscience] got to do with it?" Pavel Nikolayevich suddenly
lost his temper. "The whole idea's sheer religious rubbish! You've read too
much slush, Comrade Podduyev, you've disarmed yourself ideologically.
You keep harping on about that stupid moral perfection!"[13]

The stage is now set for a major ideological clash as Kostoglotov
confronts Rusanov. After Kostoglotov attacks Rusanov for ridicul-
ing moral perfection, the latter continues:

"If you wish to state your opinion, at least employ a little elementary
knowledge." Pavel Nikoleyevich pulled his opponent up, articulating each
word syllable by syllable. "The moral perfection of Leo Tolstoy and company was described once and for all by Lenin, and by Comrade Stalin, and
by Gorky."[14]

Under normal conditions, the invocation of such authorities as
Lenin and especially Stalin would frighten any citizen into silence.
In the cancer ward, however, with death hovering so near, fear no

longer squelches the expression of opinion. The dread threat of the disease liberates its victims politically:

"Excuse me," answered Kostoglotov, restraining himself with difficulty. He stretched one arm out toward Rusanov. "No one on this earth ever says anything 'once and for all.' If they did, life would come to a stop and succeeding generations would have nothing to say."

Pavel Nikolayevich was taken aback. The tops of his delicate white ears turned quite red, and round red patches appeared on his cheeks.....

"...I understand that Lenin only attacked Leo Tolstoy for seeking moral perfection when it led society away from the struggle with arbitrary rule and from the approaching revolution. Fine! But why try to stop a man's mouth" — he pointed with both his large hands to Podduyev — "just when he had started to think about the meaning of life, when he himself is on the borderline between life and death? Why should it irritate you so much if he helps himself by reading Tolstoy? What harm does it do?"[15]

Solzhenitsyn could not have chosen a better place than the cancer ward to discredit the flat, two-dimensional philosophy of dialectical materialism that has been drilled into the heads of Soviet citizens for decades, nor a better instrument than Kostoglotov:

"Why stop a man from thinking? After all, what does our philosophy of life boil down to? 'Oh, life is so good! ... Life, I love you. Life is for happiness!' What profound sentiments. Any animal can say as much without our help, any hen, cat, or dog.... What do we keep telling a man all his life? 'You're a member of the collective! You're a member of the collective!' That's right. But only while he's alive. When the time comes for him to die, we release him from the collective. He may be a member, but he has to die alone."[16]

From now on the ground rules of the novel are defined. *The Cancer Ward* is at heart an ideological novel concerned with man's confrontation with death, truth and falsehood. The term "ideology" must be understood rather broadly in this context, for Solzhenitsyn's question is so basic that it may be debated by both sophisticated and experienced thinkers and by the totally naive and uneducated. Podduyev's question is universal. It arises throughout the novel in various versions and contexts and elicits different responses from different individuals, depending on the experience of their generation.

The question Dr. Dontsova asks is not a direct one of the sort

Podduyev finds in Tolstoy's story, but it still concerns the same thing. The difference is that, whereas in the cancer ward patients facing death raise the question about the meaning of life in retrospect, Dontsova is discussing the future with her young, healthy son. The usual generation gap manifests itself in Dontsova's family. Her son insists that he does not intend to continue his education, that he does not wish to prepare for a profession; for that would require work, and he does not plan to spend his entire life at a job. It becomes clear that his only goal is pleasure. His values epitomize the prevailing philosophy of the younger generation formulated so forthrightly by Asya during her conversation with Dyomka:

> "Nonsense!" Asya slapped him on the back like an old friend. "Cut off your leg? They must be crazy. It's just that they don't want to treat it. Don't let them do it. It's better to die than live without a leg. What sort of life is it for a cripple, do you think? Life is for happiness."[17]

While apparently contrasting Dontsova's son and Asya, with their amazingly shallow philosophy, to Vadim, Solzhenitsyn actually places him in the same category, for he is equally egocentric. Vadim loves his profession, is a devoted worker, and studies fanatically. When with typical rudeness Podduyev interrupts Vadim's discourse on geology to point out that it is senseless to study science just before one's death and that one would do better to concentrate instead on what it is men live by, Vadim, like Rusanov, responds authoritatively: "I know the answer to that already. Poeple live by creative work. It helps a lot. You don't even have to eat or drink!"[18] When Podduyev suggests that Vadim read Tolstoy's story, the geologist protests:

> "I've already gone through it." Vadim's answer came back swiftly. "It doesn't belong to our age. It's too shapeless, not energetic enough. What we say is 'Work harder! And not just for your own profit.' That's all there is to it."[19]

Vadim's answer resembles Rusanov's: "People live by their ideological principles and by the interests of their society."[20] As these interests can be served in a Marxist society only by work, Vadim adopts Rusanov's creed, though he adds that work should be "creative." Both Rusanov and Vadim are Party members, and the former is extremely proud that he has intuitively recognized a kindred soul.

Vadim's conversation with Shulubin, however, shows that Vadim's values are as shallow as those of Asya and Dontsova's son. Shulubin, though hardly a Marxist anymore, remains a defender of the historical mission of socialism. The ideological confrontation between Vadim and Shulubin is a central episode in the plot. Shulubin interrupts Vadim's study to challenge the young Marxist idealist with a philosophical question as basic as Tolstoy's:

"Are you sure you're not kidding yourself? Do you really need all that stuff? Why that? Why not something else?"

Vadim ... answered quietly, in the same meaningful tone the old man had used, "It's ... it's interesting. It's the most interesting thing I know in the world."[21]

From Vadim's calm, thoughtful answer emerges only one reason for his preoccupation with geology — his personal interest, his fascination with the subject. Shulubin finds that justification unsatisfactory.

Shulubin introduces a new element into the discussion — the ethical value of work and creativity. Vadim in turn makes two counter-moves: he denies any relationship between science and ethics, and he even questions the relevance of ethical values. This double assault does not frighten Shulubin, however. Positing a direct relationship between science and ethical values, he defines the latter as "values directed toward the mutual illumination of human souls."[22] Shulubin gives an example of a woman working on a chicken farm under unthinkable conditions to show that in order to serve the more fortunate members of society, such as Vadim, some workers must devote their lives to labor which they could not possibly find interesting. Thus Shulubin demolishes Vadim's facile argument.

### III    *The Questioning Continues*

It is not only Vadim who is on trial, but Rusanov and the entire policy of the Soviet power structure. Vadim's answer to Shulubin's variant of Tolstoy's question is totally selfish and thus, in Shulubin's eyes, immoral. Vadim's faith in the value of science and progress is shaken by the simple example of a chicken farm worker who ruins her health in order to provide people like Vadim with three eggs daily for their breakfast. The notion that immorality is inherent in contemporary technological progress is new to Vadim, and he is completely taken aback by it. In this light his idea of creative work, not merely for one's own profit but in the service of technological progress on a purely materialistic level, conjures up a horrifying system of brutal despotism under which those who have the opportunity for creative work exploit those who do not. Furthermore, utilitarian principles determine one's worth. Solzhenitsyn shows this clearly by Vadim's astonishment at Shulubin's reference to the simple peasant woman. Why should Vadim, who does not lack for intellectual stimulation, worry about an insignificant, uncreative chicken farm worker? From Vadim's own point of view he is right. The chicken farm worker who does not contribute to technological progress is worthless and merits no attention. Shulubin, however, equates Vadim's reaction with that of the capitalist who rates men on an equally utilitarian basis, according to their contribution to the gross national product. The final, ironic remark by Kostoglotov, who had been a prisoner only a year before and is well acquainted with the conditions under which the common people must labor, points up the fallacy in Vadim's thinking.

Shulubin's response to Tolstoy's question is that one lives by creating values "directed toward the mutual illumination of human souls." In Rusanov's presence, Shulubin cannot bluntly condemn the official socialist policy of the Soviet government, which he considers as intolerable as the capitalist system. Later, however, in a discussion with Kostoglotov in the second part of the book Shulubin refines his philosophy as he continues the line of his argument on the value of technological progress which presumably will bring happiness to future generations:

"As for the so-called 'happiness of future generations,' it's even more of a mirage. Who knows anything about it? Who has spoken with these future generations? Who knows what idols they will worship? Ideas of what happiness is have changed too much through the ages. No one should have the effrontery to try to plan it in advance. When we have enough loaves of white bread to crush them under our heels, when we have enough milk to choke us, we still won't be in the least happy. But if we share things we don't have enough of, we can be happy today! If we care only about 'happiness' and about reproducing our species, we shall merely crowd the earth senselessly and create a terrifying society...."[23]

Solzhenitsyn may appear to distinguish between two generations, ascribing to the younger one to which Vadim belongs shallow and more materialistic values. Yet some of the youngsters are idealistic, and think deeply about their lives. One such is Dyomka, who appears to have a single aim in life: to break out of the trap of poverty that deprives him of higher education. He has a clear idea of what he wants to do with his life and resembles Vadim in the importance he attaches to professional training. In the final analysis, however, Dyomka's attitude is different; for he flatly refuses to compromise, to guarantee his security by entering a technological profession. He argues with Kostoglotov with laconic force, indirectly answering Tolstoy-Podduyev's question:

"Will you go to the university?"
"I'll do my best."
"You'll study literature?"
"That's it."
"Listen to me Dyomka, I'm talking seriously, you'll ruin yourself. Why don't you work on radio sets? It's a quiet life, and you can always earn something on the side."
"Oh, to hell with radio sets!" Dyomka blinked. "Truth is what I love."[24]

Dyomka's protest is as radical and significant as is Shulubin's shocking preaching of moral principles by which any progress must be measured. In a certain way Dyomka speaks for his entire generation. He speaks for Asya, who resorts to sex in part because her teachers' attempts to indoctrinate her alienate her from the very values they are trying to instill in her. He speaks also for Dontsova's son, whose educated, cultured parents could not convince him that education revealed the truth because under Stalin it obviously did not. They had to point to its professional advantages, an argument that could never convince a skeptic. Thus Solzhenitsyn defines the so-called generation gap as the refusal of the younger generation to accept the lies in which their parents were forced to live. In this context Vadim's immersion in geological research, Asya's escape into sex, and Donsova's son's retreat into the underworld appear to be escapes from the hypocrisy of the social and political structure in which they find themselves. Dyomka, however, is the most unfortunate youngster of all. His mother is a prostitute; he has had to support himself; and now his leg has been amputated. Yet he takes his stand without any compromise, declaring that one lives by searching for and serving the truth.

Rusanov's cynical daughter, Aviette, whom he dotes upon, contrasts markedly with this magnificent image of a truth-loving youth. Aviette is only a little older than Dyomka and Asya, and the same age as Vadim; but despite her youth she appears more sophisticated than her father, the old party member and secret surveillance specialist:

Was it Gorky who had said, "If your children are no better than you are, you have fathered them in vain, indeed you have lived in vain"? Pavel Nikolayevich had not lived in vain.[25]

Rusanov's reference to Gorky is laughable, for Aviette lives by a precept even more cynical than her father's:

...Generally speaking, you have to be flexible, you have to be responsive to the demand of the times. This may annoy you, Father, but whether we like it or not we have to attune ourselves to each new period as it comes![26]

Amidst the rapid political changes of the Khrushchev era, this philosophy amounted to a readiness to perpetuate one's power by any means necessary. No matter what injustices and crimes had been committed in the past, the Rusanovs and their children should continue to enjoy their privileges. Personal privileges, the good life, are for them the only values. One should erase party ideology and allegiance to the old authorities from one's mind and replace them with total opportunism. Aviette begins her formula for survival rather apologetically, but it turns out that she need not have done so. Rusanov is so petrified by the rumor that under the new system old cases may be reopened in the courts and that the MGB may even arrange confrontations between the rehabilitated and those who had borne false witness against them that he is ready for any compromise.

Aviette's philosophy links her to a grotesque character, Maxim Chaly, a black marketeer whose life is completely antithetical to Rusanov's. Nevertheless, the two men become friendly; and their relationship, based on mutual profit rather than any intellectual rapport, will doubtless endure after their release from the cancer ward. The principle by which Chaly lives is so primitive that even Aviette would be embarrassed at hearing it, but Rusanov accepts it, albeit reluctantly:

"But is it right, what you're doing?" Pavel Nikolayevich pressed him.

"It's all right, it's fine" said Maxim reassuringly. "Now have a bit of this delicious veal. We'll guzzle some of your compote in a minute. You see, Pasha, we only live once, so why not live well? What we want to do is live well!"

Pavel Nikolayevich could not help agreeing with this. Maxim was quite right. We only live once, so why not live well? It was just that . . . . [27]

After all, Rusanov's daughter has said the same. One must continue to live well; one must be flexible. Chaly invokes the same principle in his own simple way:

"We'll have a good time! We'll have a good time, Pasha!" Chaly impressed it on him. His funny old face became filled with sternness, ferocity even. "Let the others croak if they want to. You and I'll have a good time!"

They drank to that. [28]

Diametrically opposed to Chaly's philosophy is that of Vadim and Dr. Dontsova. Both the geologist and the doctor are creative and well-qualified in their professions. Both are heroic, and both contract cancer in the course of their work: Vadim, through direct contact with radioactive water during his geological explorations, and Dr. Dontsova as a radiologist overexposed to X-rays. If Shulubin were to pose to Dontsova the very questions he asked Vadim ("Are you sure you're not kidding yourself? Do you really need all that stuff? Why that? Why not something else?"), doubtless she would justify her work by pointing to the needs of the suffering, those helpless in the face of imminent death. She answers Tolstoy's question obliquely as she stops by Sibgatov's bed for the last time. Their unspoken thoughts define the degree of her devotion to the healing of the sick:

"You see, Sharaf," Dontsova's eyes were saying, "I did everything I could. But now I'm wounded, I'll soon be falling too."

"I know that, Mother," the Tartar's eyes answered. "The man who gave me life did not more for me than you did." [29]

Earlier, Kostoglotov has questioned the credibility of medicine in general. Now Dontsova recalls the numerous cases of X-ray treatment which were at first successful but later yielded tragic side effects. Her painful memories may be seen structurally as an additional and indirect response to Tolstoy's question:

...she knew that she would sooner forget ... her best cases, hardest-won victories, but until the day she died she would always remember the handfull of poor devils who had fallen under the wheels. It was a peculiarity of her memory.[30]

This "peculiarity of her memory," as the narrator terms it, is nothing less than self-renunciation, total self-sacrifice in an effort to save lives. A more self-centered person would inevitably recall the successful cases, the victories over cancer, rather than the failures. Dontsova's merciless self-examination and her perfectionism elevate her chosen work from the level of a profession to great humanitarian service. At this point Shulubin's criterion for the validation of a person's work (ethical values "directed toward the mutual illumination of human souls"[31]) moves from the theoretical to the practical realm. The scene between Dr. Dontsova and Sibgatov, with its exchange of quiet looks of love and gratitude, is an ontological realization of Shulubin's theory.

Like Sibgatov, Dr. Gangart thinks of Dontsova as "mother." Spiritual guidance, the illumination of human souls as manifested in the relationship between Dr. Gangart and Kostoglotov and that between the other self-sacrificing doctors and their patients, is a central theme of the novel. Dr. Dontsova's teacher, Dr. Oreshchenkov, typifies the ideal physician. An old-fashioned family doctor and a humane representative of the public health system, he radically criticizes modern medical practice during his diagnosis of his former student. After Dontsova's departure the old man contemplates human existence in general — not as a physician but as a philosopher:

The meaning of existence was to preserve unspoiled, undisturbed and undistorted the image of eternity with which each person is born.
Like a silver moon in a calm, still pond.[32]

Dr. Oreshchenkov is both a great healer and a teacher in that he treats his patients spiritually as well as physically. His counterpart among the patients is Shulubin, who also assumes the role of spiritual teacher or leader. In agony after his operation, Shulubin talks with Kostoglotov:

"Not all of me shall die." Shulubin whispered. "Not all of me shall die."

He must be delirious.

Kostoglotov groped for the man's hot hand lying on the blanket. He pressed it lightly. "Aleksei Filippovich," he said, "you're going to live! Hang on, Aleksei Filippovich!"

"There's a fragment, isn't there? ... Just a tiny fragment," he kept whispering.

It was then it struck Oleg that Shulubin was not delirious, that he'd recognized him and was reminding him of their last conversation before the operation. He had said, "Sometimes I feel quite distinctly that what is inside me is not all of me. There's something else, sublime, quite indestructible, some tiny fragment of the universal spirit. Don't you feel that?"[33]

This is the "image of eternity" that Dr. Oreshchenkov perceives as the essence of life and compares to " a silver moon in a calm, still pond."

The chapter metaphorically entitled "Blood Transfusion" contains a parallel image in Vega's transmission of illuminating concepts to Kostoglotov and her answer to Tolstoy's question. While lying on the table waiting to receive a blood transfusion, Kostoglotov naturally stares at the ceiling, where he sees a reflection of the sun off something outside the window. The image fills him with inner peace. When his conversation with Vega reaches its climax, the narrator links the spot of light on the ceiling with the pond in Dr. Oreshchenkov's image:

The strange patch of pale sunlight on the ceiling suddenly began to ripple. A flashing cluster of silver spots appeared from somewhere. They began to move about. Oleg watched the fast-moving ripples and wavelets. He had finally realized that the mysterious flash high up on the ceiling was no more than a reflection of a puddle, a patch of ground outside the window by the fence that hadn't dried up yet. The image of an ordinary puddle.[34]

The movement of the sunbeams from the sky to a puddle on the ground and then back up above Kostoglotov's head to the ceiling, as if back to the sky again, parallels his conversation with Vega and the course of his search for the meaning of life. Their conversation is linked to Tolstoy's question through Kostoglotov's refusal to undergo hormone therapy. Zoya, the young nurse with whom Kostoglotov has flirted, has explained the side effects to him (he will become sexually impotent). Now, lying on the table, Kostoglotov considers them:

"If my life is totally lost, if I can feel in my bones the memory that I'm a prisoner in perpetuity, a perpetual 'con,' if Fate holds out no better prospect, if the only expectation I have is being consciously and artificially killed — then why bother to save such a life?

"First my own life was taken from me, and now I am being deprived even of the right ... to perpetuate myself. I'll be the worst sort of cripple! What use will I be to anyone? An object of men's pity — or charity?..."[35]

## IV  *In Search of an Ideal*

Kostoglotov is correct, of course, in the sense that the Soviet punitive system has reduced his life to the most elemental level, forcing him into perpetual exile on the edge of a desert and thus depriving him of all cultural and intellectual pursuits. Food, love of nature, the satisfaction of manual labor, perhaps friendship, sex, and a family are the only things the system could not take away from him; yet even some of these basics must be sacrificed now merely in order to survive. Kostoglotov's dilemma raises the same questions that Podduyev has asked: What makes human life meaningful? What do men live by? None of the answers that Podduyev has received — that man lives by his profession, his army ration, his salary, or even Vadim's "creative work" for the sake of technological progress — is valid for Kostoglotov. Most of the answers are too primitive, and Vadim's ideal is outside the realm of possibility; for Kostoglotov leads a life much like that of Shulubin's chicken farm worker who is exploited in the name of technological progress. In the generally accepted, materialistic scheme of things, Kostoglotov can no longer justify his existence if he is unable to have a family. Only a radical switch to another value system, the transcendence of his inflexible, materialistic philosophy of life, could spring Kostoglotov from his spiritual trap, the dead end in which he finds himself. This moment in his life is crucial. One of the most powerful passages in Solzhenitsyn's novel describes the spiritual transmittal of life-giving concepts during Kostoglotov's actual blood transfusion:

Keeping out of sight, Vega didn't start arguing with him. Instead she suddenly launched out from where she was standing: "No, it's not true! You don't really believe that, do you? I know you don't! Examine yourself

— those aren't *your* ideas, you've borrowed them from somewhere else, haven't you?''

She spoke with more force than he had heard in her voice before. It was full of wounded feeling, more than he would ever have expected....

"There must be some people who think differently! Maybe a few, maybe only a handful, but differently all the same! If everyone thought your way, who could we live with? What would we live for? Would we be able to live at all?''...

. . . . . . . . . . . . . . . . . . . . . . . . . . . . . . . . . . . . . . . . . . . . . . . . . . . . . . . . . . .

Like a stone thrown boldly from a boy's sling made out of a sunflower stem that lengthens his arm, or like a shell fired out of one of those long-barreled guns in the last year of the war, a whooshing, whistling shell shuddering noisily through the air — Oleg shot up and flew in a crazy parabola, breaking loose from everything he had memorized and sweeping away everything he'd borrowed from other people, high over the waste-lands of his life, one wasteland after the other, until he came to some land of long ago.[36]

Kostoglotov questions the very justification of an existence stripped to its fundamentals, while Vega raises the same question as a result of his despair. In her view, if everyone adopted a materialistic philosophy, society would become intolerable. This is why her question is actually a reply to Kostoglotov's previous question. When he realizes this, he completely recaptures his real self, his youth, his idealism. In this scene Shulubin's "mutual illumination of human souls" becomes a reality, for Vega is herself reborn: "She shone. She actually shone. Yes, she was that little girl from his childhood, his school friend. Why hadn't he recognized her before?''[37] The reflection of a simple puddle transfigured by the rays of the sun into a small orb on the ceiling above Kostoglotov parallels Vega's transfiguration and his own. They share this image with Oreshchenkov, who, like Shulubin, believes that a fragment of eternity must exist in every person who would preserve his humanity.

In *The Cancer Ward* the entire universe seems to participate in the struggle of a single man to achieve an existentially sound perception of the world and a true philosophy of life. The Kadmins, with whom Kostoglotov has been living in exile, had a dog named Beetle, a noble and developed creature similar to Dr. Oreshchenkov's big Saint Bernard, who almost reaches the status of a human being. These animals are more than pets or friends: they are also teachers, for in their unspoiled essence they have preserved something that most human beings have lost — dignity, respect for living things, trust in the basic goodness of man. In a flashback, Kostoglotov recalls how he had enjoyed the affection of Beetle, whom the town officials later senselessly shot. For Kadmin Beetle's arbitrary killing was a personal tragedy, the loss of a genuine friend.

After Kostoglotov is released from the hospital, he draws many analogies between the fate of Kadmins' dog, his own experiences in the cancer ward, and the world of the animals represented in the Tashkent zoo, which he visits at that point. Both the zoo and the hospital are neatly arranged, with the animals in their respective cages and the patients in their beds. It is easy to identify a particular animal by the label on his cage, just as the doctors identify a patient by his medical chart.

Reading a sign on an empty cage, Kostoglotov realizes that the same brutality which lay behind Beetle's killing also prompted someone to injure a monkey in the zoo:

The little monkey that used to live here was blinded because of the senseless cruelty of one of the visitors. An evil man threw tobacco into the Macaque Rhesus's eyes.

Oleg was struck dumb. Up to then he had been strolling along, smiling with knowing condescension, but now he felt like yelling and roaring across the whole zoo, as though the tobacco had been thrown into his own eyes, "Why?" Thrown just like that! "Why? It's senseless! Why?"[38]

Both Beetle and the monkey were injured in the eye, and Oleg reacts similarly to the two killings: "So now they had killed the dog as well. Why?"[39]

The lust to kill is symbolized in the zoo by the description of the beasts of prey and culminates in the image of the tiger, implicitly identified with Stalin'

A little further on he spotted "Mr. Tiger." His whiskers — yes, it was the whiskers that were most expressive of his rapacious nature. But his eyes were yellow.... Strange thoughts came to Oleg's mind. He stood there looking at the tiger with hatred.

In the camps, Oleg had met an old political prisoner who had once been in exile in Turukhansk. He had told Oleg about those eyes — they were not velvet black, they were yellow.[40]

The clue to this cryptogram is Turukhansk, where Stalin was

exiled after his arrest in February of 1913. In his portraits, Stalin's eyes were always shown as velvet black, but now — looking at the tiger's whiskers and yellow eyes — Oleg sees the dictator's real face. The explanation of violence, suppression, and the lust to kill need not be rational, political, or historical. The source of evil is, in fact, much simpler than sophisticated theories would have it. Solzhenitsyn dealt with the same problem in *One Day in the Life of Ivan Denisovich,* during discussion of Eisenstein's film *Ivan the Terrible* by Caesar and K-123. This film propounds the idea that political necessity sometimes justifies cruelty and terror. Yet, in identifying Stalin with "Mr. Tiger," Solzhenitsyn shifts the genesis of the dictator's brutality from the historical arena straight into the animal kingdom, thus pointing to the psychopathology of human nature.

Interrelated images link the malignancy of cancer with the horrifying bloodthirstiness of "Mr. Tiger," the symbol of Stalin and his political system. Kostoglotov's musings on the beginning of a more liberal era in the USSR stem from a philosophy of cosmic unity whereby all aspects of life are related: "For heaven's sake, it was about time! It was long overdue. How could it be otherwise? A man dies from a tumor, so how can a country survive with growths like labor camps and exiles?"[41]

## V  *The Beauty of Life*

Oleg interprets his recovery from cancer and his eventual return home on both a personal and a national level as a single triumph of good and life over evil and death. He equates the patients' malignant tumors with the spread of concentration camps all over the country. They are a disease, an aberration from the healthy state in which human beings and nations are meant to live. After all, the world is basically beautiful; and, as Solzhenitsyn's imagery suggests, nature offers hope by promising life. Two victims of disease, Dyomka and Oleg, also victims of such social ills as crime, prostitution, the concentration camp, and exile, are struck by the miraculous beauty of the power of life and the imperishable feminine principle in nature. Two passages linked metaphorically constitute the quintessence of Solzhenitsyn's philosophy and poetics.

Asya reveals the beauty and goodness of the world to Dyomka through her body, especially her breast, inwardly permeated by disease:

She pulled her dressing gown apart (it wasn't holding together anyway). It seemed to him that she was weeping and groaning again as she pulled down the loose collar of her nightdress to reveal her doomed right breast.

It shone as though the sun had stepped straight into the room. The whole ward seemed on fire. The nipple glowed. It was larger than he had ever imagined. It stood before him. His eyes could not resist its sunny rosiness.

Asya brought it close to his face and held it for him.

"Kiss it! Kiss it!" she demanded. She stood there, waiting.

And breathing in the warmth her body was offering him, he nuzzled it with his lips like a suckling pig, gratefully, admiringly. Nothing more beautiful than this gentle curve could ever be painted or sculptured. Its beauty flooded him. Hurriedly his lips took in its even, shapely contour.

"You'll remember? . . . You'll remember, won't you? You'll remember it was there, and what it was like?" Asya's tears kept dropping onto his close-cropped head.

When she did not take it away, he returned to its rosy glow again and again, softly kissing the breast. He did what her future child would never be able to do. No one came in, and so he kissed and kissed the marvel hanging over him.[42]

Kostoglotov witnesses another miracle of nature: the apricot tree:

And then from the teahouse balcony he saw above the walled courtyard next door something pink and transparent. It looked like a puff dandelion, only it was six meters in diameter, a rosy, weightless balloon. He'd never seen anything so pink and so huge.

Could it be the apricot tree? . . .

It was his present to himself — his creation-day present.

It was like a fire tree decorated with candles in a room of a northern home. The flowering apricot was the only tree in this courtyard enclosed by clay walls and open only to the sky. People lived in the yard, it was like a room. There were children crawling under the tree, and a woman in a black headscarf with a green-flowered pattern was hoeing the earth at its base.

Oleg examined it — pinkness, that was the general impression. The tree had buds like candles. When on the point of opening, the petals were pink in color, but once open they were pure white, like apple or cherry blossoms. The result was an incredible, tender pink. Oleg was trying to absorb it all into his eyes. He wanted to remember it for a long time and to tell the Kadmins about it.

He'd planned on finding a miracle, and he'd found one.[43]

These two miracles — a young woman's breast and a blossoming

72 ALEXANDER SOLZHENITSYN

apricot tree, related in shape and color — function similarly in the novel in their effect on the two characters. To the same group of life-promising and life-giving images belongs the birch tree fungus, or *chaga,* as it is called in Russian, from which a marvelous cancer-healing tea may be produced.

It is thus up to man to turn his eyes toward nature, to learn again to use it, to enjoy it, and to live by it. Then even the tiger's yellow eyes might lose their menace if only they did not remind Kostoglotov of Stalin. Despite all the horrors and injustices of society, the world on its first day of creation was good. It remains good, unless man himself corrupts it.

Solzhenitsyn's profoundly Judeo-Christian vision of the world pervades *One Day in the Life of Ivan Denisovich* as well as "Matryona's Homestead," but it is nowhere more apparent than in *The Cancer Ward.* It is in this novel set in a hospital ward permeated by the presence of death that the spiritual theme surfaces through Tolstoy's question: What do men live by? Shulubin and Kostoglotov articulate the spiritual theme most succinctly during their conversation in the garden, when they touch upon many topics important to those who have lived under Stalin. Shulubin is tormented by the question of how it could have happened, how people could have allowed themselves to be deprived of all their rights. He eliminates *a priori* Kostoglotov's conviction that human stupidity is to blame. In a brilliant discourse, Shulubin rather surprisingly concludes: "The people are intelligent enough, it's simply that they wanted to live. There's a law big nations have — to endure and so to survive."[44]

What is most confusing about Shulubin's formulation is that his implied distinction between large and small nations suggests that the smaller nations lack the will or mandate to survive, and that their continued existence is not assured. Here Shulubin seems intolerably chauvinistic, and appears not to share the genuine sympathy for the small, oppressed nations that Solzhenitsyn has expressed on many occasions throughout his works: in his description of the two Estonians in Ivan Denisovich's brigade; in his portrayal of Sibgatov, a Crimean Tartar whose small nation Stalin brutally uprooted after the Second World War; and finally in the author's appeal to the Soviet government in his letter of September 5, 1973, to grant self-determination for all national minorities in the USSR as well as in the entire socialist bloc.

What then does Shulubin mean by his shocking distinction

between large and small nations? His ambiguous statement is difficult to comprehend. Perhaps Solzhenitsyn believes that large nations are more seriously threatened by such a despot as Stalin, driven by a messianic megalomania, especially in this era of unlimited, computerized possibilities of electronic surveillance of an entire population as large as that in the USSR. An additional disadvantage of the large nations is their military might, especially in the atomic age when dictatorships in such countries are virtually immune to any outside subversive force. Dictatorship in a large country, supported by sophisticated police and military power, is to all intents and purposes indestructible and thus may endure over a long period of time. In this light one may better understand Shulubin's seemingly paradoxical statement that the large nations have an instinctive drive to survive in any situation. One may also comprehend why Solzhenitsyn in his letter to the Soviet government advocated the reduction of the size of the country and the restriction of its armaments as steps towards increased freedom and democracy.

The conversation between Shulubin and Kostoglotov then moves to socialism as a political and economic system. Shulubin asks Kostoglotov whether he did not betray his allegiance to socialistic ideals and begin to sympathize with capitalism while he was serving his term in the labor camps. Kostoglotov responds rather vaguely, but remarks on his admiration for the affluence of capitalistic societies. Shulubin counters:

"You know, that's a philistine's way of reasoning. It's true that private enterprise is extremely flexible, but it's good only within very narrow limits. If private enterprise isn't held in an iron grip it gives birth to people who are no better than beasts, those stock-exchange people with greedy appetites completely beyond restraint. Capitalism was doomed ethically before it was doomed economically, a long time ago."[5]

It would, of course, be ludicrous to compare Stalin's version of socialism to capitalism on an ethical basis. Shulubin, however, has developed his own solution to the dilemma during his long years of seclusion. Having been afraid to talk to anyone, he discusses his unorthodox ideas for the first time only on the eve of his death. His alternative to both the brutality of Stalinism and unfettered capitalism is a new type of socialism that Kostoglotov would term Christian socialism. Shulubin decides to label it — rather modestly — "ethical socialism":

We have to show the world a society in which all relationships, fundamental principles and laws flow directly from ethics, and from them *alone*. Ethical demands must determine all considerations: how to bring up children, what to train them for, to what end the work of grownups should be directed, and how their leisure should be occupied. As for scientific research, it should only be conducted where it doesn't damage morality, in the first instance where it doesn't damage the researchers themselves. The same should apply to foreign policy. Whenever the question of frontiers arises, we should think not of how much richer or stronger this or that course of action will make us, or of how it will raise our prestige. We should consider one criterion only: how far is it ethical?[46]

There is an imprint of Tolstoyian thought upon Shulubin's utopian vision of socialist society which is also reminiscent of certain passages in Solzhenitsyn's letter to the Soviet government. *The Cancer Ward,* autobiographical though it is, is in reality a philosophical work; and its spiritual overtones are more emphatic than those of any other novel Solzhenitsyn has written.

Spiritual ideas assume many different forms in *The Cancer Ward*. One of the most important among them is the notion of conscience. It has already been shown that after reading Tolstoy's short story, the brutal and unscrupulous Podduyev begins to realize that his conscience is not clear, that he has hurt many people unnecessarily. One of his especially painful recollections concerns a young boy digging a trench along with other convicts. Podduyev compels them to continue their work despite the fact that they are completely drained of strength. The boy warns him, "All right, chief. It'll be your turn to die one day."[47] Now that day has come, and the boy's words, re-echoing in Podduyev's mind, haunt him.

Podduyev's mention of his bad conscience naturally irritates that loyal Marxist Rusanov, who denies its very existence but whose own conscience still torments him in his sleep. Rusanov's nightmares differ from Podduyev's memories only in that Podduyev recognizes their true nature. Thus Solzhenitsyn claims that conscience does exist and influences human beings whether they want to believe it or not. The objective, independent existence of conscience — which may be the strongest and most overt spiritual idea in the novel — is central to the main motif, Tolstoy and Podduyev's question: "What do men live by?"

## CHAPTER 4

# The First Circle

I  *The Uppermost Depths*

*T*HE *First Circle* represents a new step in Solzhenitsyn's artistic
development. It also poses a new problem, that of life in a
contemporary, industrialized, highly controlled society. The scope
of the novel is so enormous as to be unsurpassed in Solzhenitsyn's
previous works. The setting of *The First Circle,* unlike his first two
novels, is not confined to one place or one particular group of
characters. In *One Day in the Life of Ivan Denisovich* Tyurin's
recollections of his youth and Shukhov's reminiscences of his life at
home and his arrest are the only cases in which the narrative
extends beyond the limits of a concentration camp. The depressing
sense of confinement in *The Cancer Ward* vanishes only in the last
two chapters, when Kostoglotov leaves the hospital and wanders
through Tashkent. The atmosphere and the setting of these particular chapters, however, contrast sharply with the rest of the novel.
These narrow spatial limits — also typical of Solzhenitsyn's short
stories — are abandoned in *The First Circle,* although the main setting still remains an isolated area of confinement. The Sharashka, a
special prison in the Mavrino Institute, is a kind of technological
think-tank, an instrument for the sophisticated exploitation of prisoners by the government. The novel begins, however, not in the
prison, but in very exclusive quarters: the office of a diplomat,
Innokenty Volodin. In the course of the action the scene shifts to
the office of Abakumov, the head of the MGB (secret police) and
its vast network of prisons and concentration camps. The reader
visits an apartment belonging to the state prosecutor Makarygin;
the bedrooms of Volodin and Major Roitman, a secret service officer; the office of the research director at Sharashka, Colonel
Yakonov; a dormitory at Moscow State University; a simple village

and the forests of Byelorussia; and other miscellaneous places. The narrative also takes the reader into the most carefully guarded office of the omnipotent ruler of the empire, Generalissimo Stalin. Thus the reader both scales the heights of political power and descends to the depth of enslavement by the state. The novel is constructed on two parallel axes, the one descending, imposing Stalin's will on the entire country; the other ascending, and paralyzing that same power. While the first axis originates in Stalin's personality, the second does not emerge from any tangible source. Its genesis is to be found in the spiritual domain.

The plot of *The First Circle* is far more complex than that of any of Solzhenitsyn's completed works. A young Soviet diplomat, Volodin, tries to warn his old family doctor that he faces charges of treason for promising to share the fruits of his research with two French physicians. The MGB records Volodin's telephone conversation with the doctor's wife and sends the tape for analysis to the scientific institute in Mavrino, a prison populated almost exclusively by scientists and engineers including the protagonist, Nerzhin. Their current project is a telephone coding system ordered by Stalin. The uses of knowledge, power, and pressure by guards and prisoners, dictator and henchmen alike form the basis of the struggle for survival and integrity inside Mavrino and in the highest echelons of government as well. The prisoner-engineers identify Volodin's voice, and he is arrested. Nerzhin wins his spiritual struggle by refusing to cooperate with the Stalinist regime and heroically accepts his fate — transfer to a harsher concentration camp.

The title of the novel refers to Dante's carefully structured Inferno in *The Divine Comedy*. In Chapter 2, "Dante's Idea," Rubin explains Sharashka (and the novel's title) to a prisoner recently transferred from a concentration camp and bewildered by the "luxury" he discovers here:

"No, dear sir," said Rubin, "you are, just as you were previously, in hell. But you have risen to its best and highest circle — the first circle. You ask what a sharashka is? Let's say the concept of a sharashka was thought up by Dante. Remember that Dante tore his hair trying to decide where to put the wise men of ancient times. It was a Christian's duty to toss those pagans into hell. But the Renaissance conscience couldn't reconcile itself to the idea of enlightened men being packed in with all sorts of sinners and condemned to physical torture. So Dante thought up a special place for them in hell."[1]

The arbitrariness of the transfers of the prisoners from a lower stratum of hell to the first circle illustrates their vulnerability before a power structure that can improve or worsen their lives by whim and at will. The concept of the inferno as an autonomous kingdom with its own laws and principles is also involved here. When the character Pryanchikov remarks that "it has been proved that a high yield of wool from sheep depends on the animals' care and feeding,"[2] he provides a more prosaic explanation of Sharashka than Rubin and adds a purely utilitarian dimension to the picture.

Though the prisoners associate the empire of the MGB with Dante's Inferno, this idea expands to include ultimately the entire country and Stalin himself. Thus in the same sense that *The Cancer Ward* is not a typical medical story, neither can *The First Circle* be termed merely a novel of prison life. It is rather a horrifying indictment of totalitarianism, which achieves its most poignant expression of the twentieth century in the USSR. The few historical facts that Solzhenitsyn incorporates into the novel are the only reminder that he is offering a realistic picture of life only twenty-five years ago, still easily within the memory of this generation, in a country just a few thousand miles away — half a day by jet. Without this evidence, one might regard the novel as an anti-utopia similar to Eugene Zamiatin's *We* or George Orwell's *1984*.

The simple plot resembles that of a detective story. Volodin, a diplomat, receives information that his former family physician, Dr. Dobroumov, has promised to share the results of his medical research with some French colleagues. The MGB, having learned of this agreement, considers it treason and begins to set a trap for Dobroumov. At great personal risk Volodin telephones the physician to warn him. Despite Volodin's precaution of using a public telephone booth, his voice is recorded during his short conversation with the doctor's wife, and the tape is later taken for analysis to the technological institute, Mavrino, which is staffed by prisoner-scientists. When samples of telephone conversations of other members of the Ministry of Foreign Affairs who could have known about he Dobroumov affair are compared with the recorded warning, it becomes clear that the voice on the tape belongs either to Volodin or his associate Shchevronok. A major general of the MGB, Oskolupov, satisfied with this result, decides to arrest both suspects. Rubin, the prisoner who has analyzed their voices, is shocked by Oskolupov's decision:

"But one of them is not guilty!" Rubin exclaimed.

"What do you mean, not guilty?" Oskolupov asked in astonishment, opening his green eyes wide. "Not guilty of anything at all? The security agents will find something; they'll sort it all out."[3]

On the following day Volodin and Shchevronok are arrested and face sentences of ten to twenty-five years in a labor camp.

Oskolupov's suggestion that no man is entirely innocent and thus not liable to arrest is the point at which the novel departs from the realm of the detective story. After all, with such an attitude, the authorities can arrest all suspects, regardless of who the guilty party is. The Soviet code of justice and the notion of crime and guilt are totally alien to the Western and pre-Revolutionary Russian concepts of a human being, his rights and duties, his integrity and freedom, his significance and value. This radical rejection of all the principles of European civilization makes the world described an anti-utopian projection of mankind's nightmares onto reality. In Solzhenitsyn's novel, however, reality itself is a nightmare.

It is Solzhenitsyn's depiction of a vertical section of society that allows him to introduce this anti-utopian element into the *The First Circle*. The presentation of Sharashka alone would show the system of suppression from the same angle as *One Day in the Life of Ivan Denisovich,* although the prisoners struggling for their inner freedom and self-respect would be more intellectual than Ivan Denisovich. It would not yield a complete picture of a society built on a horrifyingly primitive value system; for, regardless of how large a segment of society a prison or concentration camp consumes, it remains a deviation from the norm. There still exists a world on the other side of the barbed wire where people manage to live a more normal life.

In *The Gulag Archipelago,* Solzhenitsyn extends the scope of *The First Circle* to include Stalin's entire empire. If one thinks of the whole country as the Inferno, then the first circle, Sharashka, is paradoxically its freest part. However, the precise nature of the relationship between the first circle and the rest of the country is not clear at the beginning of the novel, although the mere hint of such a relationship implies that Solzhenitsyn is dealing with far more significant problems than the penal system in Stalin's empire. The prison filled with intelligent, talented, knowledgeable, innocent people controlled by their intellectual inferiors bears eloquent testimony to the unparalleled stupidity of Stalinist despotism that is immediately apparent and continually stressed throughout the novel. This paradox creates the impression of an anti-utopia even as the book reflects a historical reality.

Stalin imposes his style of life and his mode of thinking not only upon the labor camps and prisons, but upon the country's entire bureaucratic machinery. Senselessly he forces his own insomnia upon the state bureaucracy in Moscow:

> Four o'clock did not mean the end of the working day but of its day-time, or lesser, part; everyone would now go home to have dinner and take a nap, and then, from ten o'clock on, thousands of windows in sixty-five Moscow ministries would light up again. There was only one person, behind a dozen fortress walls, who could not sleep at night, and he had taught all official Moscow to keep vigil with him until three or four in the morning.[4]

Stalin's intellectual impotence is companion to the enormous pomposity which conceals his basic vacuity. Solzhenitsyn's portrayal of Stalin in Chapters 18 through 21 at first appears humorous, but gradually humor gives way to horror as Stalin's personality is further revealed and finally emerges as grotesque. One of the first things one notices about the Stalinist system is its shocking lack of taste flavored with *kitsch*. The state-enforced idolatry of Stalin has inundated the country with worthless art and has contributed to the deterioration of the taste of the nation, especially among its youth:

> On the ottoman reclined the man whose likeness had been sculpted in stone; painted in oil, water colors, gouache, sepia; drawn in charcoal and chalk; formed out of wayside pebbles, sea shells, glazed tiles, grains of wheat, and soy beans; carved from ivory, grown in grass, woven into rugs, pictured in the sky by squadrons of planes in formation, and photographed on motion picture film ... like no other likeness during the three billion years of the earth's crust.[5]

This is Stalin's language, cast in a style of endless and fruitless enumeration totally devoid of any dynamic thought — an intellectual stalemate. One may easily suppose that Stalin himself here is imagining all the colors and different materials used to glorify him in portraits. One may assume that it is again Stalin who ponders with satisfaction the various ways his name permeates the world and will someday resound throughout the universe:

This man's name filled the world's newspapers, was uttered by thousands of announcers in hundreds of languages, cried out by speakers at the beginning of the end of speeches, sung by the tender young voices of Pioneers, and proclaimed by bishops. This man's name was baked on the lips of dying prisoners of war, on the swollen gums of camp prisoners. It had been given to a multitude of cities and squares, streets and boulevards, palaces, universities, schools, sanitoriums, mountain ranges, canals, factories, mines, state and collective farms, battleships, icebreakers, fishing boats, shoemakers' artels, nursery schools — and a group of Moscow journalists had proposed that it be given also to the Volga and to the moon.[6]

Solzhenitsyn's parody of Stalin's style — blending as it does in the narrative with the dictator's internal monologues — clearly indicates that the author does not regard the propaganda operation for the exaltation of Stalin as a mere political device; rather it was Stalin's own invention, employed for his self-glorification. Thus one cannot offer even a partial political justification for such vulgarity. The psychopathology of the despot is the driving force behind the gigantic propaganda machine. It is his insanity that produces innumerable portraits and requires the ceaseless repetition of his name.

Stalin's insatiable craving for glory and admiration is also sinister, for those who refuse to worship him, those who refuse to abide by his policies, are exterminated. The dimensions of his self-exaltation and his persecution of real and imaginary enemies are equally insane. A man transformed into a deity is condemned to isolation and loneliness, and Stalin's natural suspiciousness has mushroomed into paranoia over the years. Throughout his vast empire, the people feel its effects as strongly as does his immediate circle. In his private life Stalin's precautions create the atmosphere of a prison around him, and this spreads like cancer all over the country. His cruelty permeates his nocturnal discussion with MGB minister Abakunov:

Stalin was terrifying because one mistake in his presence could be that one mistake in life which set off an explosion, irreversible in effect. Stalin was terrifying because he did not listen to excuses, made no accusations; his yellow tiger eyes simply brightened balefully, his lower lids closed up a bit — and there, inside him, sentence had been passed, and the condemned man didn't know: he left in peace, was arrested at night, and shot by morning.[7]

Kostoglotov in *The Cancer Ward* sees those same yellow eyes in the tiger at the zoo, as Stalin's bloodthirstiness is likened to that of a beast of prey that metaphorically becomes an agent of death:

*Death* was the only reliable means of settling accounts in full. And when his lower lids squinted, the sentence which shone in his eyes was always *death.*[8]

Kostoglotov's astonishment at the senseless creulty exhibited in the blinding of the monkey at the zoo, and his scream, "Why? It's senseless! Why?"[9] resound in the four chapters of *The First Circle* dealing directly with Stalin, who is equally senseless and equally cruel. All the unimaginable cruelty which one finds in the novel is easily traceable to Stalin, and yet he remains as inexplicable as the genesis of evil in the world.

Stalin's straightforward acceptance of his own bloodthirstiness forms an additional link between him and "Mr. Tiger" in *The Cancer Ward.* Both are killers *par excellence,* and neither tries to conceal the fact (Stalin at least does not hide it from those in his immediate circle). Stalin's murderous instincts led the prisoners in his concentration camps to dub him with an appropriate nickname:

"Hey, kids, it looks like the old cannibal has kicked the bucket..." — "What did you say?? — "I'll never believe it" — "About time!" and a chorus of laughter. Bring out your guitars, strum your balalaikas![10]

In *The First Circle,* Stalin's blood lust has become an ethical standard by which his close associates think and act, and thus support the murderous instincts of their master:

"How we need capital punishment! *Give us back capital punishment, Iosif Vissarionovich!*" Abakumov pleaded with all his heart, putting his hand to his chest and looking hopefully at the swarthy-faced Leader....

"One day soon I will give you back capital punishment," he said thoughtfully, looking outward, as if he were seeing years into the future. "It will be a good educational measure."[11]

Stalin has created a truly vicious circle by following the practice of murdering his real and imagined enemies despite the abolition of capital punishment. His chief hangman, Abakumov, accepts this practice unquestioningly, and now begs his master to legalize execution again. Though the reinstatement of capital punishment will jeopardize the lives of both Stalin and his henchmen, how can the master resist? Immediately he cruelly offers the gift of capital punishment to his pupil:

"Aren't you afraid you'll be the first one we shoot?"...
"Iosif Vissarionovich! If I deserve it...If it's necessary...."
"Correct!" Stalin said with a smile of goodwill, as if to approve his quickness of wit. "When you deserve it, we will shoot you."[12]

While seemingly enjoying a harmonious exchange, these two men who worship the same idol — senseless murder — are actually playing a suicidal game. What Stalin asks Abakumov, the latter has already asked himself in reverse:

Of course, Abakumov understood by now that in his zealous enthusiasm he had climbed too high. To have stayed lower would have been less dangerous. Stalin spoke pleasantly, good-naturedly, with those well removed from him. But there was no retreat once one had become an *intimate.*
The only thing left was to wait for death. One's own. Or....[13]

The theme of death linking Stalin with Abakumov makes four swift turns and finally circles back to its initiator, Stalin, as the cult of death threatens eventually to devour its creator.

What occurs in Stalin's secluded study is reflected in the ranks of the bureaucracy. At night Abakumov convenes the high officials of the MGB: Deputy Minister of State Security Sevastyanov; the Head of the Special Equipment Section of the Ministry of State Security, Major General Oskolupov; and the Chief of Operations at the Mavrino Institute, Colonel of Engineers of State Security Yakonov. As they walk through Abakumov's enormous office, these three high-ranking officers pass by a picture of Stalin which stands approximately sixteen feet high. The scene in Stalin's office where death plays the role of protagonist is now repeated.

Under threat of execution, these officers commit themselves to an unrealistic deadline for the completion of the complex research at the Mavrino Institute that will lead to the production of a new coding system for Stalin's telephone. Stalin's paranoia is the sole reason for this endeavor: he must have complete secrecy. It is also obvious that in the Soviet state everything exists under the threat of death. Given his intellectual limitations, however, Stalin is incapable of understanding that nature cannot be forced to yield her secrets to scientists even though they do conduct their research under threat of execution.

The chain reaction started in Stalin's study reverberates on down through the ranks. Sevastyanov threatens both Oskolupov and Yakonov with imprisonment; Oskolupov informs Yakonov that he is well acquainted with the latter's tarnished record, that it could easily justify his swift elimination. Leaving the building at night, Yakonov drives aimlessly through the darkened capital, and stands for a while on a quay overlooking the Moscow River, obviously contemplating suicide.

But life continues, and the next day Sevastyanov and four generals bring the taped telephone conversation between Volodin and Dr. Dobroumov's wife and the tapes of three other voices to the Mavrino Institute for identification. The practical application of the new science of phonoscopy, invented by the prisoners, immediately gives rise to unnecessary arrests and insane sentences.

Stalin's effect on human relations extends further down the administrative ranks. Yakonov and Major Roitman fear each other, and Roitman later feels even more threatened when he learns that anti-Semitism is spreading throughout the country under the guise of anti-cosmopolitanism. Moreover, two security officers — Shikin and Myshin — each of whom is suspicious of the other, control the personnel of the Mavrino Institute. Hired technicians given charge of the laboratories, usually young graduates from technological schools, must attend Major Shikin's orientation lecture:

> They were told that on this assignment it was worse than being at war, that they had come to a snake pit where one careless move would confront them with destruction. They were told that they would encounter here the dregs of the human race, people unworthy of speaking the Russian language.[14]

A long line of security officers reflects Stalin's paranoia. In the same way that his quarters are ludicrously over-protected, so too is the security system of his prisons grossly exaggerated:

> No zek had the right to stay one second in his workroom without the supervision of a free employee because prudence dictated that the prisoner would be bound to use that unsupervised second to break into the steel safe with a lead pencil, photograph its secret documents with a trouser button, explode an atom bomb, and fly to the moon.[15]

This obsession with security creates an airtight system which allows only the most ingenious and courageous to escape. In general, in the world described by Solzhenitsyn either escape or open resistance is unthinkable. Just as Abakumov, both in Stalin's presence and elsewhere, feels totally controlled by his master, so does every officer, every guard, and every prisoner. The very titles of the chapters describing Volodin's arrest "Abandon Hope, All Ye Who Enter Here" and "Keep Forever" point to the fact that Stalin's system aims for nothing less than total control over the bodies and souls of men.

The spy network embraces not only the ordinary citizenry, but the convict world as well. From among the prisoners Major Shikin recruits his informers, some of whom are known to their fellow inmates, though others remain undetected. The most devoted and feared informer is the ex-officer of the MGB, Siromakha, who stands at the bottom of the chain of men supporting Stalin's dictatorship. Solzhenitsyn links Siromakha closely to Stalin by comparing the informer to a leopard, an image obviously related to "Mr. Tiger."

## II  *The Momentum of the Bureaucracy*

The anti-utopian quality of *The First Circle* becomes particularly apparent when Solzhenitsyn exposes the absurd lengths to which the ambitions of a secret police officer can lead him. Major Shikin decides that the final results of the prisoners' research are not the only worthy object of foreign espionage, but that preliminary drafts and casually discarded scrap paper may also be revealing. Final reports are locked in a safe until the security officers submit them to the authorities and burn the rest of the work sheets, but Shikin is concerned because this system fails to encompass countless pages of trial calculations and diagrams. In order to prevent an American spy from retrieving such a piece of paper from a trashbasket and dispatching it to the Pentagon, which would immediately realize what the Mavrino Institute was working on, Shikin contemplates issuing to the prisoner-scientists individual copybooks with numbered pages for their daily calculations and diagrams and then locking them in safes overnight as well. This inspired routine would eliminate the need for trashbaskets, assure that the security system is airtight, and provide Shikin the means to control his prisoners' thoughts, ideas, time, and effort. He would no longer merely be checking the truthfulness of the prisoners' statements, rather he would be determining what the prisoner-scientists were actually thinking. Realizing that an ignorant security officer would be evaluating their thoughts and that failure to produce daily calculations would lead to the conclusion that they were preoccupied, not with their research but with something else (presumably with plans to escape or to pass secrets to foreign agents), the prisoners would automatically use a certain number of pages in their draft books every day, and thus continually generate scrap paper.

Apart from the stupidity and futility of Shikin's scheme, Solzhenitsyn is really probing the major's assumption of responsibility not only for the prisoners' deeds, but for their thoughts as well. No longer merely a security officer, he assumes the role of a priest guiding the thoughts of his flock. Thus Stalin's dictatorship ominously reshapes itself into a theocracy administered by sacerdotal sergeants wearing MGB uniforms instead of clerical robes. Stalin, himself a kind of high priest, would doubtless have fully approved of Shikin's ridiculous plan to check on the daily creativity of his prisoners.

Solzhenitsyn's description of Stalin reading his own biography underscores the complete harmony between the omnipotent ruler and the modest MGB major. Whereas Shikin monitors his prisoners, Stalin brainwashes his citizens through his biography:

> Very good. And they said it was selling well. Five million copies of this second edition had been printed. For such a country that was too few. The third edition should be ten million, perhaps twenty. It should be sold directly to factories, schools, collective farms.[16]

The glorification of Stalin requires extensive indoctrination. The nation must love him. The thoughts and emotions of every human being must be channeled solely toward adoration of the ruler. To this end Stalin's biography is printed in enormous quantities and in a convenient format. Anyone can read it; the language is simple; the print is large.

How can a totalitarian regime obtain absolute control over the creative life of a nation that once produced great literature but now churns out mediocre, barely readable fiction? Solzhenitsyn suggests an answer to this painful question in *The Cancer Ward* when an obviously well-educated orderly with refined manners explains to Kostoglotov why she prefers French to Russian literature. In contemporary Russian novels she finds only lies and a humiliating underestimation of the reader's intelligence. In The First Circle, Solzhenitsyn develops this theme in detail: he almost anatomically dissects the creative process in a gifted writer, Galakhov (who resembles Konstantin Simonov, a prominent Soviet novelist and poet), whose very imagination is subject to Stalin's censorship:

> Whenever he began some big new work, he would be fired up, he would swear to his friends and to himself that this time he would not make any concessions to anyone, this time he would write a real book. For the first few pages he would work away with enthusiasm. But soon he would notice that he was not writing alone; that the presence of the person he was writing for always loomed over him; that he was involuntarily rereading every paragraph with that person's eyes. That person was not the reader, fellow man, or friend; not even the critical fraternity in general — it was always that most important critic, the celebrated Zhabov. . . .
>
> So, paragraph after paragraph, Galakhov would try to anticipate Zhabov's objections and adapt himself to them; and the book would roll out, duller and duller, falling obediently into place.
>
> By the time he was halfway through, Galakhov would see that his book had quietly changed, that once again it wasn't working out.[17]

Major Shikin's issuance of notepaper to the scientists and Zhabov's ideological analysis of literature are identical in their effect. Both pressures force the creative individual to labor under a self-imposed censorship pervading every aspect of his life. It is not any lack of knowledge or even the fear of possible persecution which makes writing an honest book virtually impossible; rather it is the way the totalitarian state conditions one to sense the constant presence of a stern observer supervising one's thoughts and feelings. Whoever the immediate observer may be, ultimately it is Stalin himself who keeps watch over the country and all its people with his yellow eyes. There is no escape. The system of external and internal surveillance is seemingly airtight, allowing no one to escape the omnipresent and omnipotent sovereign. This system creates the claustrophobic atmosphere in which Solzhenitsyn's characters are forced to interact.

Solzhenitsyn's novel requires a certain effort on the part of the Western reader to imagine the lives of its characters, whether or not they are behind prison walls. The situations in which these characters find themselves are incomparably more hopeless than those ever experienced by most Westerners. This dissimilarity can be explained by the differing principles of governing various nations. Normally it is the law that delimits the freedom of the individual. In Stalin's empire as Solzhenitsyn presents it, however, the individual must follow strict orders as to what to do, think, and feel — under penalty of death.

### III   *The Vulnerability of the System*

The system is not airtight, though. Stalin's elaborate police state remains in the end vulnerable, its control less than total. The episode involving Doronin illustrates the limits beyond which the regime cannot extend its control. Even the "king of stool pigeons,"[18] Siromakha, feels threatened as soon as he discovers the plot of his recently recruited colleague, Doronin, to expose all the informers. The most important element of Doronin's gamble is precisely its irrationality, its almost suicidal quality which makes it unpredictable and thus almost uncontrollable by Major Shikin, who has recruited Doronin.

The MGB pays its informers monthly with money orders sent by fictitious persons. Doronin capriciously chooses to receive his payments from a nonexistent Klava Kudryavtseva:

They asked me in whose name they should send it. They said, "Would you like it from Ivan Ivanovich Ivanov?' The cliché jarred me. So I asked, 'Couldn't you send it from Klava Kudryavtseva?' After all, it's nice to think that a woman cares about you.[19]

Were Major Shikin a better psychologist, he would recognize Doronin's unreliability in his rejection of the clichéd name in favor of a feminine "donor." A more perceptive officer would realize that this prospective informer has imagination, a certain creative flair, and thus a measure of unpredictability; but such perceptions are too refined for such a bureaucrat as Major Shikin. Furthermore, it would be unrealistic to suppose that the MGB, with its millions of agents, could exclusively recruit discerning personnel. Inevitably it must utilize the services of men of even lower intelligence than Major Shikin. Furthermore, the massive spy system which requires an enormous number of agents necessitates a large and inflexible bureaucracy. As it would be very expensive to bill the MGB for the postage, every informer receives his monthly payment of 150 rubles minus the cost of the postage, or three rubles. That awkward sum of 147 rubles which no one is likely to receive as a gift brands every informer. Doronin plans to expose all the agents in Sharashka by drawing attention to this unusual amount of the personal money orders they receive on payday.

The combination of the MGB's bureaucratic brainlessness, unavoidable in an operation of this scope, and the sense of adventure inborn in certain people who, despite their unsuitability for the job, are nevertheless recruited by undiscerning officers, together produce the scandal instigated by Doronin. Ironically Siromakha, who reports Doronin's exposé of the informers, had been before his arrest an MGB officer whose adventurousness led to crime and imprisonment.

The unpredictability of the individual is the greatest threat to the MGB, as it is also to Stalin and to his entire regime. If the nation consisted only of people like Shikin, Stalin's empire would be perfect. Among the basic human traits which prevent this is man's sense of humor, his love of laughter. Doronin, for example, substitutes for the official slogan, "The country must know its heroes," a parody of it: "The country must know its secret agents."[20] This has a double, humorous effect — as a parody and also as a contradiction in terms. Doronin is called into Shikin's office, is beaten, and is threatened with execution, but he has already inflicted damage on the spy network in Sharashka.

The system is deficient on a higher level as well. The supposedly insurmountable wall separating the prisoners from the young, female laboratory supervisors begins to crack. Simochka, Nerzhin's supervisor, falls in love with him, is willing to bear his child, to wait for him, and, most importantly, to conceal the book which he is secretly writing during his working hours, to smuggle it out of prison, and to keep it for him until his release. Simochka's behavior is as instinctive as Doronin's: the difference is only one of motivation. Doronin's exposure of the informers grows out of his sense of adventure, mischief, and boredom while Simochka's devotion to Nerzhin and her betrayal of the MGB stem from the most elemental of human feelings, the sexual instinct. The grave shortage of men in the USSR after World War II has left the homely Simochka with no prospects of marriage. It is absurd to entrust the supervision of a laboratory staffed with youthful, brilliant, and vigorous men to a young, unmarried girl such as Simochka; yet the simplistic methods of the MGB, which repeatedly ignores the human factor, present her with the very temptation that leads her to commit a crime and betray her employer. By the end of the novel she has already had one abortive love affair with a prisoner; from now on no psychological barrier remains between her and the men in Sharashka. The laws of nature are beyond even Stalin's power to control.

Far more threatening to the Stalinist system is Doronin's romance with Clara Makarygin, the MGB supervisor. The lack of female companionship is a great frustration to Doronin, and his affection for Clara parallels that of Simochka for Nerzhin. Unlike Simochka, Clara is an attractive member of a privileged family, has many opportunities for love and marriage, and is simply sorry for an obviously gifted young man without a chance in life. Gravely transgressing the MGB code, she listens to his story and is moved by the persecution and cruel ruin of an innocent man. Thus it is not only the sex drive which endangers the established system but the more profound and refined human qualities — in this case the almost forgotten feeling of compassion — that are virtually impossible to control.

Even the home of Makarygin, a major general of the MGB, is not immune from dissident ideas. Under Doronin's influence Clara raises embarrassing questions of justice and ethics that by tacit agreement were simply not asked by those who benefited from Stalin's regime. Ironically it is Doronin, that nonentity of Stalinist society, who indirectly unsettles the MGB prosecutor with unlimited power over the prisoner. Doronin may die in a labor camp, but Clara will live with her questions, and the prosecutor will not forget that he has been subjected to very painful and embarrassing inquiries and accusations from his own daughter, over whom he cannot exercise his judicial authority.

It would be wrong, however, to ascribe Clara's ideological transformation to Doronin alone. Solzhenitsyn describes her growing political awareness and her spiritual development very carefully. The crucial moment in this process is related in a flashback to the time when Clara learns that her family's new apartment building has been constructed by convict labor. Ascending the staircase to inspect her new apartment, the well-dressed Clara passes by a female convict washing the floor:

The charwoman, who could not bear that silk or that perfume, remained bent over; then she looked up to see whether there were more of them.

Her burning, despising glare turned Clara to ash. Streaked with splashes of dirty water, she had the expressive face of an intellectual.

Clara experienced not only the shame one always feels in passing a woman washing the floor, but, seeing her patched skirt and her padded jacket with cotton wool sticking out of the rents, she felt a still greater shame and horror. She froze there and opened her purse. She wanted to turn it inside out and give it to the woman, but she did not dare to.

"Well, pass!" the woman said angrily.[21]

Since that time Clara almost religiously avoided walking on the steps that this woman washed! Her look was more expressive and revealing than any words could have been. The words come later, after Clara's sister Dotnara marries a young diplomat, Innokenty Volodin. On that same staircase, Clara asks her brother-in-law a question which has tortured her ever since she saw the woman prisoner washing the steps and which she cannot ask anyone else. Volodin's answer ("Little Clara! So you're beginning to figure things out!")[22] spurs her spiritual development: Clara's political conversion is a crucial point of the novel. The brief moment when she catches the look on the prisoner's face encompasses a total metamorphosis in the prosecutor's daughter and yet is outwardly so inconsequential that no police system in the world could possibly have prevented it.

The only instance in which Solzhenitsyn directly addresses his reader is significant in this connection:

The zek puts his hands behind his back and, four abreast (one step to the right or left and the guard will open fire without warning), surrounded by dogs and guards, he goes off to his railroad car.

You have all seen him at the railway station at that moment, but in your cowardly submissiveness you have averted your eyes and turned away. Otherwise the lieutenant in charge might suspect you of something and take you into custody.[23]

Despite the complete hopelessness of this situation, which individual protests could not alter, one must still read this passage as a reproach to Solzhenitsyn's fellow Russians, who are neither tyrants nor prisoners but humiliated traitors forced into silence and passivity under a reign of terror.[24] This passage adds depth to Clara and to her reactions to the world around her. Indeed, if Clara's new vision is generated by the look on one prisoner's face, what must other Russians think and feel as they see rows of convicts sur-

rounded by guards and dogs? Clearly then, as Shulubin intimates in
*The Cancer Ward,* people are intelligent enough to understand that
the horrors being perpetrated are excessive, that the connection
between legal justice and the punitive system in Stalin's state is
non-existent. Such a realization must arouse definite anti-Stalinist
feelings, unexpressed though they may be, in at least part of the
population.

## IV    *The Individual versus the Apparatus*

The failure of Stalin's ambitious system to take cognizance of the
human factor is apparent in the higher echelons of the administration as well. On three separate occasions in Yakonov's office the
secret police confront a single, defenseless prisoner: Sologdin,
Nerzhin, and Gerasimovich. In all three cases the prisoners emerge
victorious, and the MGB is defeated. Just as the motives behind the
prisoners' struggles vary, their victories differ qualitatively.

In Sharashka a prisoner's life can follow one of three courses. In
the event of an unfortunate development in his research, or for
disciplinary or political reasons, a prisoner may face the abrupt ter-
mination of his relatively secure existence in the Mavrino Institute
and transfer to a labor camp. A preferable alternative is to stay as
long as possible at Mavrino though, as a rule, the prisoners are
delivered to labor camps a year or so before their terms end. The
best that can happen is to score a significant enough success in
one's research to win amnesty and release from prison, which usually means complete rehabilitation. The scientists are for the most
part forced to work under the pressure of the first and third
alternatives (a whip and carrot system) that require all their skill
and ingenuity.

Sologdin,[25] a brilliant mathematician quietly working alone on
the crucial telephone coding project for Stalin's personal use, is the
only one who achieves a definitive breakthrough. Sologdin's fellow
prisoner, Professor Chelnov, an authority in the field, praises
Sologdin's solution of the problem and suggests that he deserves
release for it. Sologdin tells Chelnov he has no intention of handing
his invention over to the authorities even though it may purchase
his freedom. In his view, it is immoral to supply Stalin and his
government with additional instruments of oppression. Sologdin,
therefore, places his drafts among other papers that are to be
destroyed and then watches from the window as they are burned in

the courtyard. When he is called to Yakonov's office, it seems that Sologdin has decided not to cooperate with the government.

As it turns out, however, he has made a brilliant gamble. After receiving Chelnov's approval for his design, Sologdin destroys it, and thus protects himself against Yakonov's using it without his consent. When Sologdin informs Yakonov of the plans' destruction, the latter is psychologically stripped of his defenses, for his life depends upon the successful completion of the project by Stalin's unrealistic deadline. Sologdin's coldblooded gambit reverses the roles, enables him to acquire control over Yakonov's life and death, to become, so to speak, another Stalin for the moment; while Yakonov, who represents Stalin's power within the limits of Sharashka, is temporarily Sologdin's helpless prisoner:

> "I don't understand.... It's suicide — I don't understand." ... This was not the colonel of engineers speaking, but a desperate, worn-out, powerless being.[26]

Yakonov's despair identifies him with his prisoners in Sharashka. Just as Sologdin's life was threatened earlier, so Yakonov's is now in danger:

> "You played a risky game, my friend. After all, it could have ended otherwise."
> Sologdin spread his hands lightly. "Hardly, Anton Nikolayevich. It seems that I estimated the institute's position and your own quite accurately. Of course, you know French. *Sa Majesté le Cas!* His Majesty Opportunity! Opportunity rarely passes close to us; one has to jump on its back in time, and squarely in the middle of its back!"[27]

A sudden jump on the middle of a victim's back typifies the tiger, Solzhenitsyn's consistent symbol for Stalin. "His Majesty" who "rarely passes close to" a prisoner is also a part of this metaphor which reverses the roles of the prisoners and the authorities. When "His Majesty" (not only chance, or opportunity, but also the authorities) comes within the reach of a prisoner, the latter may utilize the same methods by which he has been previously victimized. The victory now belongs to the otherwise entirely powerless but daring Sologdin.

His triumph, though brilliantly achieved, nevertheless degrades him in his struggle against Stalin's dehumanizing dictatorship. Sologdin wins personal freedom, but the price he must pay is very high. He fully realizes what kind of device he has agreed to give the authorities; he is aware of the immorality of his collaboration with the MGB; and he knows that such compromise is spiritually destructive. Despite his differences with the Marxist Rubin, in the past both have conscientiously refused to pay the price the authorities demand for one's freedom — total submission to and collaboration with the Stalinist regime. Yet now Sologdin deliberately sells out to the authorities by inventing another instrument of suppression for them. His brilliant victory is thus the utter spiritual defeat of submission to Stalin's system. In this light, Solzhenitsyn's metaphor equating Sologdin with a beast of prey acquires a double meaning: that of power in the world of primitive violence on the one hand and, on the other, his descent to Stalinist standards.

Nerzhin's confrontation with Yakonov is a victory of a higher spiritual and ethical order. Nerzhin is of central importance in the novel, not only because of the nature of his problems and the amount of text devoted to him, but also because of his drive to comprehend the tragedy of his country under Stalin's dictatorship. Despite Nerzhin's scientific education, he is primarily concerned with humanitarian questions, and carefully conceals in his desk a contemporary history that he is writing in microscopic script.

When Yakonov offers to transfer Nerzhin from acoustics research to the more important cryptography laboratory, Nerzhin refuses. He realizes that the transfer would entail a drastically increased work load: up to fourteen hours of exhausting calculations daily. Nerzhin rejects the temptations of comfort, food, and relative security for intellectual freedom — time to think, to meditate — and thus remains faithful to his values.

Once again Nerzhin is tempted: this time the bait is personal amnesty and reestablishment in Moscow. His reaction illustrates another side of his character in view of the fact that the opportunity for thought and observation is uppermost in his mind. One might assume that release from prison and reestablishment in Moscow would be the most appealing bait Nerzhin could be offered; but again he refuses, not so much for personal as for political reasons:

"They'll remove the conviction from my record!" Nerzhin cried angrily, his eyes narrowing. "Where did you get the idea that I want that little gift? 'You've worked well, so we'll free you, forgive you.' No, Pyotr Trofimovich!" And with his forefinger he stabbed at the varnished surface of the little table. "You're beginning at the wrong end. Let them admit first that it's not right to put people in prison for their way of thinking, and then *we* will decide whether we will forgive *them*."[28]

Nerzhin's reply shows that he is both a dedicated thinker and a potential political leader guided by principles of justice.

The third and last confrontation in Yakonov's office is that between Gerasimovich and the head of the special equipment section of the MGB, Major General Oskolupov. A knowledge of Gerasimovich's past is important here for an understanding of his behavior in Yakonov's office. Not long after Gerasimovich's marriage and graduation, he was arrested and was sent to Siberia. His was the destiny of a man with particularly bad luck, one with the appearance and manners of a prerevolutionary intellectual whose mere presence irritated the average Soviet citizen and aroused suspicion in the 1920's. Despite Gerasimovich's looks, however, he was uninterested in politics and philosophy and did not pose any threat to the government. After a string of misfortunes in Siberia and the loss of two children, he and his wife returned to Leningrad just before the outbreak of World War II and the German blockade of the city. At this point, Solzhenitsyn distinguishes Gerasimovich from others in his same predicament. Working as a gravedigger to keep from starving during the siege of Leningrad, Gerasimovich used to accept as payment the traditional piece of bread from the family of the deceased, though they were usually starving themselves. The emotional and human implications of this payment by bread in a besieged and starving city are enormous, but Gerasimovich lacked moral strength. Embittered over his ruined career and life, he "found an excuse for himself: 'People wasted precious little pity on us; we won't waste pity on them!'"[29]

Gerasimovich displays a completely different attitude in his short conversation with his wife. On the verge of a nervous breakdown, she begs him to produce some invention for the government to secure his release and to ease her intolerable life. He discourages her, for he is no longer willing to ensure his own well-being at the price of other people's suffering. It is not the Gerasimovich of Leningrad, but an entirely new man who rejects Major General Oskolupov's proposition.

Oskolupov's horrifyingly simplistic offer and his description of the projects on which Gerasimovich would work (microphones concealed in park benches to record private conversations and cameras to photograph objects in the dark) carry the unmistakable

Stalinist imprint and epitomize the anti-utopian grotesquery of the novel. Considering the offer, Gerasimovich recalls his wife, her exhaustion, and her plea that he obtain his release from prison. Oskolupov, continuing to urge the project upon him, insists, "It's right in your field,"[30] but suddenly the episode takes a surprising turn:

> ...Gerasimovich stood up...
> "No! That's *not* my field!" he said in a clear high voice. "Putting people in prison is not my field! I don't set traps for human beings! It's bad enough that they put *us* in prison...."[31]

Of the three prisoners — Sologdin, Nerzhin, and Gerasimovich — only the first derives any practical benefit from his interview, and even he does so at the cost of complete spiritual capitulation to the Stalinist regime. Nerzhin clings bravely and consistently to his intellectual freedom and stands firm in his dedication to the freedom of his nation. Heroic resistance by a man with no hope of survival, however, is the course chosen by the prisoner who outwardly appears the weakest of the three — Gerasimovich. His final words to Oskolupov sound like a refusal not only to collaborate with the MGB, but even to live in a country in which microphones are hidden on park benches where lovers sit and the police watch every citizen day and night on the streets and in doorways. Gerasimovich's refusal — which shocks Yakonov — represents the highest development of Solzhenitsyn's ethical system.

Ascending the ladder of Stalin's hierarchy, the reader enters the enormous office of the minister of State Security, MGB General Abakumov, where there are again three confrontations — two with prisoners and the third with high MGB officers. The prisoners, Pryanchikov and Bobynin, both brilliant engineers, have strikingly different personalities. Pryanchikov is an eccentric and witty young man totally out of touch with reality, a carefree dreamer, an inventor full of ideas and visions, and totally unpredictable. Bobynin is a middle-aged man of great intelligence and will power, which provide him an advantage in dealing with the MGB.

Abakumov's conversation with Pryanchikov ends in failure. The minister of State Security, who is under pressure to meet Stalin's insane schedule for the production of a telephone coding system, confronts a man who breathes physics and mathematics and to whom the mention of a one- or two-months deadline is simply laughable. Pryanchikov is so deeply immersed in his research that any administrative or political considerations seem ridiculous to him. He tries to enlighten the ignorant Abakumov as to the problems the engineers face by explaining the complex theory of sound waves. Thus Abakumov, and by extension Stalin himself, is challenged not by human beings, whom he can control and crush, but by nature's physical laws, indeed the very structure of the universe which is beyond the power even of a dictator to control. Ironically, it is the most naive and impractical prisoner in Sharashka who causes Abakumov to face the intractability of nature.

Bobynin's clash with Abakumov is strikingly different. Employing intelligence and the will to resist as checks upon Stalin's authority, Bobynin replies to Abakumov's threat as brazenly as Gerasimovich had refused Oskolupov:

"We would make you talk."

"You are wrong, Citizen Minister!" Bobynin's strong eyes shone with hate. "I have nothing, you understand — not a thing! You can't get your hands on my wife and child — a bomb got them first. My parents are already dead. My entire property on earth is my handkerchief; my coveralls and my underwear that has no buttons—" he demonstrated by baring his chest — "are government issue. You took my freedom away long ago, and you don't have the power to return it because you don't have it yourself. I am forty-two years old, and you've dished me out a twenty-five-year term. I've already been at hard labor, gone around with a number on, in handcuffs, with police dogs, and in a strict-regime work brigade. What else is there you can threaten me with? What can you deprive me of? My work as an engineer? You'll lose more than I will. I'm going to have a smoke."[32]

The responses of Pryanchikov and Bobynin complement each other much as do those of the three prisoners in Yakonov's office. The system with its visions of absolute power over man and nature is ultimately completely powerless precisely because of its absolutism. There is a fundamental difference between ruling by organizing and guiding people and ruling by tyrannizing over them. The latter method is clearly shown to be self-defeating. One constantly confronted with the threat of death may choose the freedom of suicide and cease to obey orders just as nature herself refuses to fit herself to man's requirements.

## V    *Stalinism and Its Faithful Servants*

Bobynin's reply — that Abakumov cannot restore freedom to a

prisoner, since he, the minister of State Security, does not possess it himself — raises the reader to the next level of understanding the totalitarian system as presented by Solzhenitsyn. For further analysis, one must return to Stalin's office from whence this survey of the totalitarian social structure began. For a better comprehension of the events in Stalin's study, one must remember the prisoners' tactics of complicating issues, delaying production, and stretching out deadlines as a defense against the inhuman pressures of the MGB. Before radically rejecting Oskolupov's proposal, Gerasimovich seriously considers accepting the new assignment and then quietly sabotaging it. Solzhenitsyn emphasizes this defensive technique throughout the novel very often, associating it so specifically with the prisoner mentality that one does not expect to find such tactics used by others. Nevertheless, the three high MGB officials employ precisely this strategy of deception and covert resistance when they confront Abakumov. Sevastyanov, Oskolupov, and Yakonov each has his own excuse and his own complicated version of the situation to present to Abakumov in order to relieve the pressure and win some extra time, just as the prisoners do with their bosses.

Back in Stalin's office, the same game continues. This time, however, the trick cannot succeed, for Stalin has pushed Abakumov to the wall, and retreat is no longer possible. Almost paralyzed by terror, Abakumov avoids looking at the telephones on Stalin's desk for fear that they may attract the despot's attention and remind him of the secret telephone coding system promised but still not ready. During the entire, lengthy session with Stalin, Abakumov carefully skirts the dangerous topic. Thus does the faithful servant deceive his master. (Yet ironically, during that same conversation, Abakumov readily consents to his own execution should he deserve it, or should Stalin desire it.) In Abakumov's own office he has been a victim of the same tactics he has just employed himself. Only after the departure of the "three liars" does he realize that his subordinates have tricked him. Stalin realizes the same about Abakumov after their meeting.

Abakumov, the brazen fellow, had sat there a good hour, the dog, without saying one single word about it!

That was the way they all were, in all the organizations — every one of them tried to deceive the Leader! How can you trust them? How can you *not* work at night?[33]

And so it goes, in a vicious circle.

What can Abakumov say to Bobynin when presented with the harsh fact that the jailer himself has been jailed? Evidently the entire country, from the dictator's office down to the strictest concentration camps, is one enormous prison, in which the inmates of Sharashka paradoxically possess a higher degree of inner freedom than Stalin himself. Thus the Dantesque metaphor in the novel's title has a double function. Sharashka, the freest place in the country, is not merely the highest circle of the prison world, but of Stalin's entire empire. It is in Sharashka that Rubin mocks Stalin's judicial system by staging a mock trial of Prince Igor and Potapov tells the story of Mrs. Roosevelt's visit to a prison camp, "Buddha's Smile." Only a prisoner could ridicule the system so savagely and escape punishment. In terms, then, of the freedom to express oneself, to be candid with one's friends, to discuss issues of the greatest importance such as the historical tragedy of Russia and the role of the individual in this tragedy — Sharashka is unquestionably the first circle of hell.

Sharashka is a paradoxical place in another respect as well. Unbeknownst to Stalin, one of his most fervent admirers, Rubin, is incarcerated here. An erudite philologist, a man of great idealism and intelligence, Rubin is nevertheless a dogmatist devoted to dialectical materialism and Marxism. So strong are his beliefs that he refuses to recognize the reality of his own tragedy and that of his fellow inmates. It is tragic and at the same time comic that a man such as Rubin, stripped of every human right by Stalin's regime, still follows with fascination the progress of the civil war in China, coloring in the territory that Mao Tse-Tung's forces have taken until the entire map of the country is red. In Rubin one sees how the Stalinist system destroys its most valuable servants.

Dedication of itself does not fully qualify one to serve a tyrant: evidently mediocrity is a far more important prerequisite, as the ignorant Party secretary Stepanov so aptly demonstrates. The gifted Rubin does not measure up in this regard and must be kept behind barbed wire; for talent and intellect are as unpredictable as humor, the sexual instinct, a sense of adventure, or even stubbornness, which, as Solzhenitsyn shows, turn out to be the most effective weapons against Stalin's tyranny.

For all Rubin's intellect, however, he, like Sologdin, has an ideological blind spot. Although he refuses to serve as an informer in Sharashka, Rubin performs essentially the same villainous task by identifying the voices on the tapes supplied him by the MGB. However, while Sologdin agrees to collaborate for his own selfish reasons, Rubin is sincerely committed to the Marxist cause. Their collaboration constitutes the most poignant tragedy of Sharashka.

Rubin's idealism links him with Nerzhin. Despite the fact that they are of opposing political beliefs, they enjoy a precious friendship. Both possess brilliant and inquisitive minds, though Rubin's commitment to Marxism severely limits his intellectual horizon. Rubin's inquisitiveness makes him a voracious reader, while Nerzhin's sole passion — to learn the truth about his country, to understand Russia's historical tragedy — accounts for his fascination with people, and particularly the simple Spiridon.

## VI *Common Sense and Intellect*

One should bear in mind that Russian society after Peter the Great (1672–1725) experienced a widening schism between the educated and the uneducated classes. As Western culture entered society solely through education, the masses did not enjoy its benefits. The privileged educated classes, on the other hand, deprived of contact with the populace, felt morally obliged to share their cultural assets with the people. Most important, the educated classes, cut off from the majority of the nation, tried to approach and understand the peasants, with their unique mentality and philosophy. This, of course, is a considerable oversimplification. Not every educated Russian in the nineteenth and early twentieth centuries was, in fact, interested in understanding the lower classes, nor did every Russian belong to the radical intelligentsia. In general, however, this division within the nation played a very important historical and political role for almost a century and a half, as the attraction of certain members of the intelligentsia to the lower classes significantly contributed to the elaboration of revolutionary ideologies in Russia. This attraction also left its imprint on Russian art, and especially literature. Some members of the intelligentsia regarded the uneducated classes as the most reliable source of that wisdom needed to solve the social and political crises plaguing the Western world and to function as the basis for an ideal social structure.

With this background one can better understand why this simple man, Spiridon, and his heartbreaking story intrigue Nerzhin so. Spiridon, who knows instinctively what he must do in every crisis, is devoted to his immediate family and to his land. Abstractions have no part in his thinking; he is interested not in the entire nation, or in mankind in general, but only in his own family — his wife and children, the basic element of society — and his land. Spiridon could not care less about the vast territory of Russia. His homeland is the field that feeds him and his family. He desires only to cultivate it, regardless of political or historical conditions. His unshakable common sense so impresses Nerzhin that the latter probes for Spiridon's views on a more theoretical problem: the justification of violence utilized in the interests of progress, justice, and peace. Spiridon's reply in the form of a proverb is amazingly quick, simple, and pointed: "The wolfhound is right, and the cannibal is wrong!"[34] The Russian version — *volkodav — prav, a lyudoed — net!* — throws more light on the proverb. The phrase contains two compound words: *volkodav* ("wolfhound") consisting of *volk* ("wolf") and *dav* ("killer," in this case) and *lyudoed* ("cannibal") composed of *liud* ("people") and *ed* ("eater," in this case). Thus the Russian words for "wolfhound" and "cannibal" rendered respectively into English would be wolf-killer and people- or man-eater. So Spiridon's formula literally reads: "The wolf-killer is right, but the man-eater is not!" or "Those who destroy wolves are right, but those who destroy people are not!"

The Russian compound words in this proverb also imply a closer relationship between wolf and cannibal than is apparent in the English text, for a wolf can also kill human beings and thus become a *liudoed,* or man-eater. Both compound words contain the notion of violence and destruction. Spiridon does not advocate peace, or even avoidance of violence. He justifies both violence and killing, but only if they serve to protect human life. The implications of this proverb are clearly political, for the prisoners repeatedly refer to Stalin as *lyudoed,* a cannibal. The wolf, synonymous with cruelty, injustice, and senseless suffering, also recurs throughout Solzhenitsyn's works. In *One Day in the Life of Ivan Denisovich* the name of the cruelest officer in the camp, Lieutenant Volkovoy, is derived from the word for wolf.

Thus Spiridon's proverb is in full accord with his philosophy of life that values above all else the most basic and irreplaceable elements of human existence, the family and its piece of land. He calls for the destruction of those who threaten human life, who take away one's land, whatever their political or philosophical orientation may be. Spiridon's philosophy is so fundamental as to be beyond the reach of any political rhetoric; it renders him, like millions of unsophisticated Russians, invulnerable to Stalin's brainwashing tactics. Nature herself seems to speak through Spiridon as he formulates his principle for Nerzhin. This scene parallels that in which Pryanchikov confronts Abakumov with the stubborn laws of physics that are not subject to Stalin's apparent omnipotence.

Though from an entirely different cultural background, the character Agniya is as unalterably opposed to Stalin's ideology as the practically illiterate Spiridon. Agniya is introduced in a flashback when Yakonov is shown walking alone at night through Moscow. In despair after his meeting with Abakumov, Yakonov suddenly finds himself on a hill covered with broken bricks, the remnants of an ancient church, and recalls that Agniya, a fragile girl seemingly detached from reality, foresaw the destruction of this ancient church and the general deterioration of his life.

Agniya's family, members of the Russian revolutionary intelligentsia, taught her from early childhood that the oppressed, the weak, and the deprived must be helped and protected and that the oppressor and exploiter must be resisted or destroyed. These basic principles of the nineteenth-century Russian radical intelligentsia were, of course, presented to her with political labels fastened to them. The underdog was the lower classes, the workers and the peasants; the oppressor was the tsar and his government, the privileged classes, and the Russian Orthodox Church, which the revolutionaries generally viewed as a pillar of the tsarist regime. Yet after the establishment of the Soviet government all these political labels became meaningless to the perceptive and analytical Agniya. The tsar and his family were executed, and the privileged classes either emigrated or were harshly persecuted by the new regime. The church suffered a tragic fate as well, for the faithful were systematically annihilated. Agniya sees the basic principles of the nineteenth-century revolutionary movement in their nakedness, stripped of all labels and rhetoric. With fresh perceptions, she seeks out the oppressed who need her help and the oppressors whom she must oppose. Paradoxically, the new regime — founded on the same ideology on which Agniya was reared — has now suppressed the church. The roles have been reversed. By those same principles that once inspired attacks on the church, it now deserves help and defense. Thus Agniya, whose family is loyal to the Soviet regime, becomes a dissenter. As she cannot support the current policies of the government nor approve of her fiancé Yakonov's future career,

she presumably joins those whom the power structure is persecut-
ing — the Christian believers and the active members of the Church
— and her relationship with Yakonov ends.

Agniya possesses enormous willpower and an outstanding intellect. At the same time, she obviously does not esteem comfort or
security above all else and totally disregards the trivial values so
important to the average person, including Yakonov. She is not
particularly attractive physically, nor does she try to be. Her powerful and independent intellect, her upbringing in the old, heroic,
revolutionary tradition, and her total contempt for material things
combine to make her extremely dangerous to the regime. She is as
immune to political propaganda as Spiridon and Nerzhin, though
for different reasons. She is prepared to fight for justice like an old
Russian revolutionary, no matter what the cost; and she has
nothing to lose, for she wants nothing for herself. In this respect
she resembles Bobynin, who concludes that a man with nothing to
lose is free. She also shares with Spiridon unshakable values and
firm ties to the old Russian traditions.

Solzhenitsyn depicts the clash between the revolutionary tradition of the Russian intelligentsia and Stalin in a passage in which
the dictator visits the Museum of Revolution on the twentieth anniversary of the socialist revolution:

In one of the halls — the same one in which the enormous TV set now
stood — he had seen as he entered two large portraits high on the opposite
wall. The faces of Zhelyabov and Perovskaya were open, fearless, and
they cried out to all who entered: "Kill the tyrant!"

Stalin, struck by their twin stares as by two shots, drew back, wheezed,
coughed. His finger shook, pointing at the portraits.

They were removed immediately.[35]

Andrey Zhelyabov and Sofya Perovskaya, members of a revolutionary underground group called the Land and Freedom Party,
organized the assassination of Tsar Alexander II on March 1, 1881,
and were subsequently arrested and executed. The daring and courage of the assassins inspired successive generations of Russian revolutionaries fighting for the rights of the lower classes; yet their
message stripped of passing political labels represents a threat to
Stalin, the so-called leader of the working class. The young revolutionary Perovskaya, like Agniya, belonged to the privileged classes.
Perovskaya was born into the nobility; Agniya, into a revolu-

tionary, elite family. Yet for emotional, ethical, and humanitarian reasons Agniya, like Perovskaya, turns against the establishment that shields her privileges, and against the tyrant — whoever he may be.

To the metaphor of hell employed for Stalin's repressive regime, Solzhenitsyn counterposes the transcendental power of good, which at least partially negates the dictator's authority. This indestructible, positive force, barely recognized during times of peace and security, becomes the hope of an entire nation, and by extension of all mankind, during such tragic times as the Stalinist era. By demonstrating the innate power of goodness to preserve the best in the human spirit, *The First Circle* shows us that the individual can triumph spiritually over a totalitarian regime.

## CHAPTER 5

# Short Stories

S OLZHENITSYN'S short stories and novels written roughly
over the same years are closely linked with one another philo-
sophically. There is, however, a significant difference between the
three novels and the short stories. At least two of the novels deal directly with prison life, and the third, *The Cancer Ward,* alludes to it
through the figure of Oleg Kostoglotov; in his short stories
Solzhenitsyn does not concern himself with this feature of society.
There he seems rather to be attempting to break out of the context
of forced confinement in order to project his ideas and philosophy
in a more familiar setting. And yet even Solzhenitsyn's short stories
do not omit the experience of the *zek* altogether. "Matryonin
Dvor" (Matryona's House) and "Pravaya Kist'" (The Right
Hand), both highly autobiographical, contain veiled references to
the convict's world. The narrators of these stories are better able
than the average man to evaluate the injustices of the social structure and life in general, presumably because of their experience in
the labor camps. In Solzhenitsyn's short stories, prison life is thus
no longer a major topic in itself, but an experience which engenders
in his characters a more profound view of the world.

## I  *"Matryona's House"*

"Matryona's House," or, more literally translated, "Matryona's
Homestead," is a story about the drab life of a remote village
which has long been a *kolkhoz,* or collective farm. The simple plot
can be summarized in one sentence: a former prisoner, now a
schoolteacher, moves into the village, rents a room in Matryona's
log cabin, becomes acquainted with her and her brother-in-law (her
first fiancé), and later learns of her death in a train accident.

Because it is set in a *kolkhoz,* "Matryona's Homestead" has
usually been interpreted as a reflection of that dismal rural life

resulting from Stalin's collectivization of the countryside. Such an interpretation, however, ignores most of the text. The story is rather about Matryona herself and offers a profound portrait of her personality. One of Solzhenitsyn's most striking achievements in this story is his artistic economy in depicting an apparently insignificant human being who finally attains such spiritual heights that she emerges as the only righteous member of her community. Matryona certainly does not attract anyone's attention, and only one whose perception has been sharpened by suffering would recognize any appealing or remarkable traits in this elderly woman.

To this end Solzhenitsyn draws on his own experience to create the narrator, Ignatich, who stands apart from the people around Matryona. He holds a university degree and teaches mathematics in high school. Though we know little about him, his point of view is clear. He was apparently an army officer arrested during World War II, sent to a concentration camp for several years, and later exiled to the edge of a desert near the periphery of the USSR. Weary, he now seeks silence, simplicity, and the beauty of nature. He has not returned from exile in the wilderness to enjoy the excitement of a big city but rather to lose himself in the forests of central Russia, where the uncorrupted language and the traditional way of life are untouched by modern civilization and are still closely linked with the past. This is why in the market place he quickly arrives at an understanding with a simple woman, whose local dialect flavored with melodic intonations attracts him.

Ignatich does not wallow in self-pity, but is content to lead a spartan life provided he is not disturbed by the tasteless instruments of modern urban civilization, such as the village loudspeaker. What allows Ignatich to look beyond the trivialities and vanities so important to the average person is his extraordinary perceptiveness acquired in passing through the most horrible experiences known to man — war and concentration camps. This is essential to the story's development. Ignatich's prior experience enables him not only to adjust quite readily to the extremely primitive life on Matryona's homestead, but also to appreciate her simple, peaceful, and harmonious personality, her spiritual strength, and her genuine, unshakable love for everyone and everything.

Matryona stands apart from the other rural people in the story, who are basically possessed by overwhelming greed. The ancient, ubiquitous, and hopelessly primitive instinct to acquire, to protect, and finally slavishly to augment their own property is the villagers' dominant drive. Matryona is an icon of dignified poverty, unique in her community. She is a spiritual outsider, perhaps not even aware of her uniqueness, having never contrasted her own philosophy with that of her neighbors and relatives.

If we compare Matryona to the usual positive hero portrayed in the works of socialist realism, we may discern an interesting twist in Solzhenitsyn's choice of a protagonist lacking the basic drive to acquire private property. The new, socialist man as presented in the Party-controlled literature is also emancipated from the acquisitive impulse, but not because of its obvious senselessness. Rather he struggles fanatically for technological progress, and is dedicated to collective acquisition. The accumulation of property remains the common denominator of the old and the new man, except that the owner of that property changes. It could not be otherwise, given the fact that the old capitalist and the new socialist ideologies both place their faith in technological progress, with its ability continually to increase the production of material goods.

Matryona, however, does not acquire material goods because she does not believe in their value, and this very lack of belief enables her to transcend all political systems and governments. The question that she raises by her way of life is universal, relevant to all centuries and all nations: should an individual devote his life to material acquisition, or is there not something more important worthy of human attention and sacrifice?

Matryona shares with socialist man an indifference to private property, but she rejects his almost religious faith in technological progress and collective ownership. She ridicules such progress in her reaction to an announcement about the invention of new agricultural machinery, as she unconsciously questions the ecological wisdom of endless technological improvement by asking where the old machines will be stored.

Ignatich's understanding of Matryona evolves gradually. Despite the fact that he is adequately prepared to appreciate her rare qualities, he still does not immediately grasp her spiritual significance. At the beginning of the story, Ignatich perceives Matryona merely as a lonely, quiet, elderly woman who is periodically ill and who is isolated from the community. Soon, however, her more essential qualities — her inner peace and her benevolent attitude toward all her surroundings — emerge through her radiant smile and naturally friendly, always polite replies. Ignatich notices that Matryona is at peace with herself and possesses the highest degree of inner freedom, since she never acts contrary to her principles. The price she pays for her freedom is extreme poverty, for she earns no money at all but derives her livelihood solely from nature. A single goat provides her with milk; she warms her house by collecting peat in the forest, which amounts to stealing from the government; she prepares preserves from bilberries that she gathers in the forest; and she cultivates her small potato garden, which supplies the main nourishment for her goat, Ignatich, and herself. During her first winter with Ignatich, Matryona's financial situation improves because she collects rent from him and receives her late husband's state pension. Her illness attacks her less frequently. She makes a winter coat for herself and puts some money aside for her funeral. She is perfectly self-contained and happy, and these very modest improvements may partly account for her improved health.

As Ignatich observes, Matryona has a rather refined esthetic sense. She likes plants and grows many in her home. She also displays good taste in music. Listening to Shaliapin's rendition of Russian folksongs on a radio program, she protests, "No. He hasn't got it right. That's not the way we sing. And he plays tricks with his voice."[1] Another time she surprises Ignatich with a genuine appreciation of a recital of Glinka's songs:

Suddenly, after half a dozen of his concert arias, Matryona appeared excitedly from the kitchen, clutching her apron, with a film of tears misting her eyes.
"Now that's . . . our sort of singing," she whispered.[2]

At the end of the story, Ignatich remembers Matryona — her enjoyment of the beauty of art and nature, of work for its own sake without any selfish calculation of profits, and her childlike, unquestioning acceptance of the people around her. She is dead and buried, and her relatives have carefully divided her meager belongings among them before Ignatich realizes how exceptional Matryona was:

None of us who lived close to her perceived that she was that one righteous person without whom, as the saying goes, no city can stand.
Neither can the whole world.[3]

Vladimir Dal's *Tolkovyi slovar' russkogo yazyka* (Explanatory Dictionary of the Russian Language) contains a similar Russian saying, the obvious source of which is Genesis 18:20-33. The adjective "righteous" which Solzhenitsyn applies to his protagonist is applicable as well to Shukhov and Alyoshka the Baptist, from *One Day in the Life of Ivan Denisovich*. These three characters resist the brutalization of man's interactions with his fellow man, reject the generally accepted way of life, and question the value of that normal life which one should supposedly preserve at any cost. They suggest that there is a limit to the price one ought to pay merely to exist. All three characters are linked by their common character to the better educated and more eloquent Nerzhin in *The First Circle*. Matryona, however, is the most vulnerable and only posthumously stands out from her dehumanizing environment. She is also the only character in Solzhenitsyn's works who endures life-long hardship outside the confines of a concentration camp or prison. For these reasons her righteousness is difficult to recognize. Even Ignatich comes to recognize Matryona's true worth only after her death and after listening to her sister-in-law criticize her. At the end of the story the reader learns that the philistine villagers had ostracized Matryona because she did not share their way of life. The righteous person is an outcast in the world Solzhenitsyn depicts. This is why it takes another outcast, an ex-convict only recently returned from exile, to recognize Matryona for what she really was.

A similar view of the world is at the core both of Matryona's philosophy and Kuzyomin's code in *One Day in the Life of Ivan Denisovich*. Matryona did not make the improvement of her material situation her chief priority. She did not raise a pig, nor did she accumulate possessions as did the other villagers, who place more value on them than on their own lives. It is as if someone like Kuzyomin had once told her something along the following lines: The *kolkhoz* dehumanizes people, but one can still retain one's dignity. The ones who become animals are those who care too much for their earthly treasures, those who forget the beauty of the world and the pure joy of being alive.

## II    *"An Incident at Krechetovka Station"*

"An Incident at Krechetovka Station" is a war story, although the war itself is not depicted. The plot revolves about an incident which in itself is rather ridiculous. An utterly unmilitary-looking soldier, Tveritinov, an actor prior to his mobilization, has become separated from his unit after breaking out of German encirclement and now, alone, is trying to overtake his original transport. He approaches Lieutenant Zotov, the commander of the railroad station at Krechetovka, for further directions.

Zotov, the protagonist of the story, is a young idealist, a patriot, and a devoted Marxist. His administrative zeal and his willingness to help wherever he can are remarkable, and in this instance he tries to aid Tveritinov. Zotov also admires literature and the theater, and this interest leads him into a warm discussion with the ex-actor.

Relaxing after their friendly conversation, Tveritinov makes a tragic blunder by admitting that he does not know the city of Tsaritsyn has been renamed Stalingrad. This causes Zotov to suspect that the odd-looking soldier is a German spy, a Russian emigré who has been dropped behind the front lines and is now roaming around in a Red Army uniform collecting military data for the Germans. On the basis of this suspicion, Zotov delivers Tveritinov to the MGB. Although Zotov later makes some inquiries, he learns nothing more of Tveritinov, and presumably fears the authorities may never release him after his arrest. Zotov cannot forget Tveritinov — "the man with the delightful smile and the snapshot of his daughter in her little striped dress. Surely he had done everything he should have done. Yes, but . . . ."[4]

One may, of course, argue that Zotov only did his duty in reporting a suspicious man to the authorities. After all, the MGB had the resources to determine whether the man really was a spy or was simply a mobilized Russian actor who never read the newspapers, was uninterested in politics, and consequently was ignorant of a particular city's change of name. The argument is plausible, however, only if one chooses to ignore entirely the political climate in the USSR at that time. Even a man like Tveritinov, removed from the mainstream of life, knows that an arrest by the MGB is almost always fatal, that one rarely returns from behind barbed wire. At the moment of his arrest he shouts at Zotov: "What are you doing, what are you doing?" . . . in a voice that rang like a bell. "You're making a mistake that can never be put right!"[5] This is why Zotov remains morally responsible for turning Tveritinov over to the secret police. The question that remains is how Zotov, with his patriotic zeal and devotion to the Party during the first unsuccessful months of war, might have found another, more flexible, and thus more human approach to the dilemma Tveritinov presents? Could Zotov have risked letting a suspicious man remain free to continue his journey through the country?

The narrator offers the key to this solution at the beginning of the story, in the course of an argument among some railroad workers about another incident at Krechetovka Station. Though only mentioned in passing, this incident is closely related to Tveritinov's case. Two trains — one carrying sacks of flour, some of which is in open cars, and the other bearing evacuated soldiers who have broken out of German encirclement and are being transported to the home front for retraining and recuperation — meet at the station. Demoralized after unusually heavy combat, the troops lack their usual discipline. During their transport they have doubtless been fed only irregularly because of conditions during the war and the bureaucratic inefficiency of the local authorities. As soon as the soldiers realize what the adjacent train at the station is carrying, they begin to steal the flour despite the warnings of a lone, young guard. In despair he fires a shot and unfortunately kills one of the soldiers — clearly unintentionally. The other soldiers on the transport are prepared to kill the guard, who is saved when an officer pretends to arrest him.

Later, in a room at the station, a retired railway worker, Kordubailo, discusses the unfortunate incident. He has voluntarily returned to work during the war, obviously out of patriotism. Two women railroad employees, Valya and Frosya, try to justify the young guard's action, but the old man, while outwardly agreeing with them, actually interprets the incident very differently:

"What else could he have done?" Valya argued, tapping her little pencil. "He was on duty, he was the guard!"

"Well, yes" — the old man nodded agreement, dropping large bits of red ash on the floor and the lid of his lantern. "Yes, that's right. Still, everybody wants to eat."[6]

The juxtaposition of two incontrovertible laws — that of the state or army, and that of the empty stomach, so cleverly introduced by the old man — creates a difficult and irritating dilemma for Valya:

"What are you on about?" The girl frowned. "What do you mean 'everybody'?"

"I mean you and me, for instance." And Kordubailo sighed.

"You don't know what you're talking about, grandad! They're not hungry, you know. They get their rations. You don't think they travel without rations, do you?"

"Well, I suppose not," agreed the old man. . . .[7]

The contradiction is clear. These presumably well-fed soldiers are stealing not delicacies or vodka but a staple, flour, which they obviously cannot transform into edible food:

"Have you girls ever tried eating raw flour mixed with water?"
"Why should I eat it raw?" Frosya was shocked. "I'd mix it up, knead it, and bake it."
The old man smacked his thick, pale lips and said after a pause — he always talked like this; his words came out lamely and awkwardly as though on crutches: "Then you've never seen hunger, my dears."[8]

Thus does the old man by indirection lay bare the fallacy of Valya's argument. The soldiers must have been ravenous: this is the only possible explanation for their interest in the flour.

At this moment Zotov, who has overheard the conversation from his room, rushes in to uphold the Party viewpiont: "Lieutenant Zotov stepped over the threshold and broke into the conversation. 'Listen, old man, you know what taking the oath means, don't you?'"[9] Zotov injects the oath into the argument with the obvious intention of silencing the stubborn old man. However, it is precisely Kordubailo's age which negates Zotov's tactic:

The old man gave the lieutenant a bleary-eyed look. He was not a very big man, but his boots were big and heavy, soaking wet, and smeared in places with mud.
"'Course," he muttered. "I took it five times."
"Well, who did you swear the oath to? Tsar Nicky?"
The old man shook his head. "Before that."
"What? Alexander III?"
The old man smacked his lips regretfully and went on smoking.
"There you are. Nowadays they take the oath to the people. Isn't there a difference?"[10]

Clearly Zotov's argument is pure rhetoric, for many meaningless oaths have been sworn in twentieth-century Russia, which has seen several regimes come and go. Valya readily perceives the fallacy in Zotov's argument, and she quickly shifts to the seemingly more persuasive ground of so-called "people's property" in her effort to defend the young guard:

"And whose flour is it? It belongs to the people, doesn't it?" Valya said angrily, tossing back her tumbling curls. "That flour wasn't going to the Germans, was it?"

"That's right." The old man quite agreed. "But those boys weren't Germans either, they're our people too."[11]

In peacetime Valya's argument would be difficult to refute. A very simple, clear logic would operate. The country is ruled by the people; all property is the people's property; anyone who damages the people's property is the people's enemy; the people's government and its special institution, the MGB, should rid the country of the people's enemies.

In wartime, however, an additional factor distorts this line of logic. The real enemy now is Germany. That fact makes it virtually impossible to label a Russian soldier who is fighting the Germans an enemy of the people. The rhetoric of peacetime turns out to be nearly invalid in time of war. This is why Zotov, who is essentially a dogmatist, feels threatened by the old man's remark and loses his temper:

"You stupid old man." Zotov was roused. "Don't you know about law and order? Suppose we all just help ourselves — I take a bit, you take a bit — do you think we'll ever win the war?"[12]

Valya and Frosya try to help Zotov enlighten the old man.

"And why did they slice the sacks open?" Valya said indignantly. "That's no way to act. Is that what we expect from our boys?"
"But why waste it? Why let it spill out onto the track?" Frosya too was indignant. "All that flour bursting out and pouring away, comrade lieutenant! Think how many children could have been fed on it!"[13]

In any argument, the mention of "hungry children" is usually the last resort of hypocrites and demagogues. The old man, however, is too clever to be trapped by this move. He places all the blame on the authorities, who are obviously mismanaging the "people's property" just as they are mismanaging the entire war effort: "'That's right,' said the old man. 'But in this rain all the flour in those open [cars] would get wet anyway.'"[14]

The old man's remark is the last sensible comment in the argument. Zotov is deaf to the excellent lecture which Kordubailo gives him, can think only in terms of propagandistic Party clichés, and cannot learn from an old man who has taken oaths to five different governments in his lifetime and who is immune to official Party rhetoric. Zotov continues to torment himself with painful and dangerous questions:

The point was, why was the war going like this? Where was the revolution all over Europe, why weren't our troops advancing virtually unscathed against every possible coalition of aggressors? Instead, there was this mess. And how much longer would it last? ... Anguish gripped his heart at the thought that Moscow might be surrendered. Zotov never spoke his thoughts aloud — to do so would be dangerous — and he was afraid even to say them to himself. Trying not to think about it, he thought about it all the time.[15]

The narrator explains Zotov's terrifying shortsightedness, his inability to perceive reality correctly, to think for himself, and to comprehend the independent thoughts of others. His deification of Stalin has robbed Zotov of his intellectual independence, his ability to analyze life and historical events:

Vasya Zotov considered it a crime that such cowardly thoughts should even run through his head. It was blasphemy, it was an insult to the omniscient, omnipotent Father and Teacher who was always there, who foresaw everything, who would do all that had to be done and would never let it happen.[16]

Such a man as Zotov — and there were millions like him — must eventually become cruel. His fanatical faith in the official lie must ultimately bring him to a bitter conflict with someone who in one way or another would force him to face reality. Actually, Kordubailo is a good candidate for arrest, but he cleverly veils his beliefs behind a seeming imbecility. The second incident — with the oddlooking, cultured, and not-so-shrewd Tveritinov — ends tragically.

Zotov is something of a tragic figure himself. Basically a man of fine character — a patriot, a faithful husband, a diligent officer, and a student who tries to educate himself in his spare moments — he would seem nearly flawless had not the narrator purposely omitted from his description the two essential traits of common sense and humor. Frosya's naive but cheerful declaration that nothing can harm her now that she has enough coal for the winter prompts Zotov to think: "Stupid woman — got her coal and now she's got nothing to worry about — not even Guderian's tanks?"[17] His is the shortsightedness typical of a fanatic — the inability to comprehend how people can live their simple lives and not commit themselves solely to the ideas and concerns he feels are so important.

The theme of this story recalls that of *The First Circle*. In both works Solzhenitsyn exposes the inflexible fanaticism of Party members with their deification of Stalin, who in reality is the sole source of the incredible stupidity and cruelty incarnated in the bureaucratic machine. No one is particularly to blame. Zotov acts as he is expected to act in Stalin's system; the MGB functions as it must according to Stalin's philosophy. Everything operates as it should. Yes, but....

### III   *"For the Good of the Cause"*

Solzhenitsyn's "For the Good of the Cause" may appear to deal with the Soviet educational system, teacher-student relations, and the struggle among various administrations. It would be inaccurate however, to interpret it this simplistically, for certain passages would then become superfluous. Only when the focus shifts away from the school itself, with its pupils and teachers, to the struggle between Grachikov and Knorozov does its real point become clear. It is divided into six chapters, three of which serve to introduce the conflict, and three of which develop the central theme: the perpetuation of Stalinist methods of governing in the post-Stalinist Soviet Union. The first three chapters are also imbued with a cheerful, carefree, youthful spirit in contrast to subsequent events, which are hopelessly monotonous and depressing.

The story begins on the first day of the academic year at a technical school. The usual reunions between teachers and students, friendly greetings, and the sharing of news engender a special excitement this year, for the school is to move from its old building to a new one specially constructed to accommodate the students' needs. The new building has many features that the old one lacked: laboratories, spacious auditoriums, modern and well-equipped gymnasiums, a hall for cultural events and dancing parties, and finally — perhaps most essential for the students' everyday needs — dormitories. Until now the students from out of town have had to rent often inadequate rooms in private homes. The joy felt by all on this first day is due in large part to the fact that the students actually helped construct their new school and thus take a builder's pride in it.

Lidia Georgievna, the most popular teacher and the faculty representative in the school's Komsomol youth organization, had assumed a supervisory role in the students' building effort. As the students in the courtyard freely discuss the merits of various classical authors, it becomes evident that this teacher differs greatly from the one Asya describes in *The Cancer Ward*. Lidia Georgievna does not pressure her students; she merely tries to persuade them in the course of a free and spontaneous exchange of ideas. The refreshing intellectual freedom which permeates this conversation creates one of the most joyous scenes in all of Solzhenitsyn's works.

The description of the school, its teachers and students, is almost idyllic. The quality of the faculty and the student body is enviable. The students — enthusiastic, hardworking, intelligent, unselfish, well-disciplined though somewhat mischievous, completely natural and charming — by voluntarily donating their leisure time to construct their new schoolbuilding, follow one of the most admirable principles of Soviet society, that of helping oneself by working for the community. In administering the project themselves, the students have followed yet another important Soviet ideal, the self-government of the working people.

This idyllic scene soon fades, however. For all that the students clearly embody the most sacred principles of Soviet society, that same society in its official incarnation begins to work against their interests. Comrade Khabalygin, the head of a relay manufacturing plant, has persuaded the 'first secretary of the regional Party committee, Comrade Knorozov, that their city should have a scientific research institute in order to advance one step beyond the neighboring towns. Of course, this is also in the personal interest of Comrade Khabalygin, who intends to become the director of the institute. By praising the new school building, he persuades the right people in the right ministry in Moscow to locate the institute not only in the town, but in the new structure. The students are aghast at the shocking unfairness and lawlessness of the highest authorities in the town, who have cynically plotted against them.

At this point the protagonist of the story appears — Ivan Grachikov, the secretary of the town Party committee and an old friend of the school principal, Fyodor Mikheyich. When the principal realizes that his plans for moving into the new building have been thwarted, he calls on Grachikov, an unusual character in Solzhenitsyn's works, whose temperament makes him an excellent leader, a democratic and humane administrator. Of course, the democratic process moves more slowly than a dictatorship:

> Knorozov, first secretary of the regional Party committee, soon noticed this weakness ... and hurled at [Grachikov] in his irrefutably laconic manner: "You're too soft. You don't act the Soviet way." But Grachikov stood his ground: "Why do you say that? Quite the contrary. I work in a Soviet way — I consult the people."[18]

Grachikov uses the word "Soviet" in its pre-Stalinist sense, when the noun *soviet* had not yet lost its original meaning of 'council' or 'counsel'. Later the narrator underscores Grachikov's lexical perceptiveness by describing his objection to the use in everyday situations of military terminology that only arouses unnecessary hysteria:

> At the factory he had tried to break other people of the habit and had himself avoided such expressions as "advancing on the technological front" ... "we threw ourselves into the breach" ... "we forced their lines" ... "brought up reserves..." He thought that these expressions, instilling the ideas of war into peace itself, sickened people. The Russian language could manage very well without them.[19]

Perhaps the figure of Knorozov illustrates most eloquently how unique a man such as Grachikov was in Stalinist and post-Stalinist Russia:

> Knorozov was in this region what Stalin had once been in Moscow: he never changed his mind or retracted a decision. And although Stalin had died long ago, Knorozov lived on. He was one of the leading examples of the "[strong-willed]" style of leadership and considered this his own greatest merit. He could not imagine that leadership could be exercised in any other way.[20]

Solzhenitsyn shows Knorozov in action just before Grachikov enters his office to defend the school's interests. As secretary of the regional Party committee, Knorozov must also deal with agricultural problems. At this point he has just finished giving instructions to a livestock specialist:

> "Well, then," Knorozov said to the livestock expert, lowering five long, outspread fingers slowly and weightily in a semicircle onto the large sheet of paper, as if placing a huge seal on it. He was sitting up straight, without

using the back of the armchair for support, and the contours of his figure, from both side and front, seemed drawn in harsh, straight lines. "Well, then — I've told you what you must do now. And what you must do is what I tell you."

"Of course, Victor Vavilich." The livestock expert bowed.[21]

Knorozov conducts his consultation in typical Stalinist style, and his orders are accepted as if they came from the dictator himself.

It is difficult to imagine a confrontation between this small replica of Stalin and the peaceful, reasonable, humble Grachikov; and yet Grachikov displays tremendous tenacity in his resistance to injustice. An uncontrollable rage wells up inside him in such situations. As he waits outside Knorozov's office, Grachikov recalls an incident which occurred during World War II. While he was directing trucks across a river a lieutenant-general tried to enter the column out of turn:

Until he was ordered to let them through, Grachikov had been prepared to explain everything calmly, without any shouting, and might even have let them through. But when right clashed head-on with wrong and the latter was backed up by greater force, Grachikov stuck to his guns and cared nothing for what might happen to him.[22]

Solzhenitsyn's works are populated with normally peaceful men such as Grachikov who confront willful, brutal authority with equally irrational resistance. Such persons remain the only hope for society and for the individual. In the struggle for the schoolbuilding Grachikov, rising to the occasion, brings the argument around to the most sensitive topics of administrative policy and Party ideology:

"Which means more to us in the end — stones or people?" Grachikov shouted. "Why are we arguing over a heap of stones?...

"Communism will not be built with stones but with people, Victor Vavilich!" he shouted, all restraint gone. "It's a harder and longer task, but if we were to finish the whole structure tomorrow and it was built of nothing but stones, we would never have Communism!"[23]

Finally Grachikov's resolution produces results. Knorozov yields, and the two reach a partial, modest compromise. The school principal is informed that the smallest and least valuable part of the property will remain under his control. The new four-million-ruble building will be assigned to the research institute, with alterations costing one and a half million rubles, obviously a senseless waste. At the end of the story, the school has still been deprived of part of the courtyard. The authorities persist in their autocratic methods, and the only force capable of resisting them is a man such as Grachikov.

The students, with their enthusiasm for socialism and progress, are cheated twice over: their aspirations for better learning and living conditions are not met, and the cynical older generation betrays their socialist ideals. Finally Knorozov, a man whom the school principal has always admired, betrays him. Yet, ironically, the authoritative style of administration still appeals to some, particularly to those of mediocre ability, such as Mikheyich, who fall as the first victims to the rule of the iron fist.

Mikeyich's admiration for Knorozov both sheds light on the former's weakness and exposes the causes of his own defeat:

Fyodor Mikheyich drew himself up and fixed his gaze on Knorozov. He liked him. He had always admired him. He was happy when he went to his meetings and could imbibe and charge himself with Knorozov's all-embracing will power and energy. Afterwards, he would cheerfully feel like carrying out his instructions in time for the next meeting, whether it involved raising the pass rate of his students, digging up potatoes, or collecting scrap metal. What Fyodor Mikheyich liked about Knorozov was that when he said yes he meant yes, and when he said no he meant no. Dialectics were all very well, but like many others, Fyodor Mikheyich preferred unambiguous decisions.[24]

Now, after losing the schoolbuilding and meeting the bureaucrat Khabalygin, the helpless and usually meek Fyodor Mikheyich begins to exhibit some signs of protest. The final scene pits the antagonists — the principal and Khabalygin — against each other in the courtyard. Khabalygin directs the workers as they illegally redraw the boundary between the school and the future research institute to the obvious advantage of the latter. Turning to Fyodor Mikheyich, he explains:

"It must be done like this, comrade."

"Why *must* it?" Fyodor Mikheyich lost his temper and his head started to shake. "You mean for the good of the cause? Just you wait!" He clenched his fists, but he had no more strength left to speak, so he turned away and strode quickly towards the street, muttering: "Just you wait, just you wait, you swine!"[25]

Might Solzhenitsyn here be parodying the helpless, mediocre Eugene's famous threat to the equestrian statue of Peter the Great in Pushkin's *Mednyi vsadnik* ("The Bronze Horseman")? On a cold, autumn night, Eugene stands before Peter's monument and, clenching his fist just as Fyodor Mikheyich does, whispers angrily, "You just wait, you architect-wondermaker, you just wait."[26] Russian critics have often claimed that Pushkin justifies Peter's brutal Westernization of Russia and condemns Eugene's threat to the tsar and his creation. This interpretation is a total misreading of Pushkin's poem, and often stems from political rather than literary considerations. Apparently Solzhenitsyn rejects this interpretation of Pushkin's poem, if indeed this passage is a parody of it. In any case, there seems to be a clear link between these two works written more than a century apart. Both address themselves to the plight of the "little man" who must sacrifice his basic human aspirations for the putative well-being of the public or the nation, or, in other words, "for the good of the cause."

## IV   *"The Right Hand"*

Research on Solzhenitsyn's works is particularly difficult because of circumstances which limit our knowledge of his life and, more important, deprive us of any information about the history of his creative writing. We cannot review his notebooks or his early drafts of published works, as is customary in literary studies. The manuscripts of "The Right Hand," for example, would be most helpful in determining whether Solzhenitsyn originally intended to include it in *The Cancer Ward,* for one may easily imagine Oleg Kostoglotov as the "I" narrator of this story. Some interesting parallels between the two works support this assumption. Both are set in a Tashkent hospital and, more specifically, on the hospital grounds, where Kostoglotov frequently strolls while undergoing treatment and where the protagonist of the short story meets Bobrov. In both works an ex-convict living in forced exile confronts a representative of the power structure, a man closely associated with the Party. In "The Right Hand," Bobrov, a Red Army man during the Civil War, is a Party member suffering from terminal cancer.

The Kostoglotov-Rusanov relationship, however, does differ significantly from that between the narrator and Bobrov in this story. Although both Rusanov and Bobrov are loyal to the government, they are far from equally successful. Rusanov is a self-satisfied bureaucrat who has realized his highest aspirations, whereas Bobrov, homeless and shabbily dressed, is obviously unsuccessful. His hopes for treatment rest in an old, barely legible document which states:

## WORKERS OF THE WORLD UNITE!

This certificate is presented to Comrade Bobrov N.K. for active service in 1921 in the distinguished "World Revolution" Special Detachment of _____ Province for personally eliminating large numbers of counter-revolutionary terrorists.

                                        Signed: Commissar _____ [27]

Kostoglotov's hatred of Rusanov becomes increasingly obvious in every word Oleg addresses to him, but it is not always entirely clear whether this is because of Rusanov's political convictions, or his privileged position, or both. In the case of the poorly dressed Bobrov, however, the origin of the narrator's antagonism is clear. Initially the narrator is exceptionally helpful to Bobrov. Only after reading Bobrov's thirty-year-old commendation for distinguished service does the narrator leave him in the waiting room of the hospital at the mercy of a young and arrogant nurse who obviously will not help him. The narrator departs without saying goodby, without even looking back although only a few moments before he has given Bobrov three rubles from his half-empty purse. The narrator does not argue with Bobrov, as Kostoglotov does with Rusanov; but neither does he pity this obviously dying man, who helped suppress counter-revolutionary movements so long ago. The fatal disease from which both the narrator and Bobrov suffer binds them for a while; but their philosophies, and especially their attitudes toward violence, alienate them from each other and terminate their short, friendly relationship.

## V    *"Zakhar-the-Pouch"*

The search for a national tradition is completely understandable in a man such as Solzhenitsyn, who stands in diametric opposition to the present social and political structure of his country. "Zakhar-the-Pouch" is imbued with such nostalgia. Narrated in the first person, with an archaic lexicon and phraseology, the story describes a two-day bicycle excursion to the site of the fourteenth-century battle of Kulikovo, where for the first time in 150 years of subjugation the Russians managed to defeat the Tatars. This battle, the first step toward liberation from the Tatar yoke, was a turning point in Russian history. Like many events in Russian history, the battle required almost more stamina than the country possessed. The casualties on the Russian side were so heavy that the Tatars, despite their defeat, maintained their control over the country for another century. Nevertheless, for every Russian the battle of Kulikovo is a powerful national symbol.

Solzhenitsyn builds his story by contrasting the significance of the battle with the inadequate measures taken to protect the battle site against theft and vandalism. The visiting narrator describes the present site in somewhat ironic tones, alternating with a romantic pathos as he recreates the past in his mind. The author's idyllic nostalgia, obviously rooted in his rejection of the present, naturally directs his sympathies to the romanticized past, where he hopes to find guidelines for solving contemporary problems.

## VI   *"The Easter Procession"*

At the beginning this story appears to be built on an antithesis between the loyal members of the Russian Orthodox Church, who proclaim their faith despite governmental persecution, and the barbarous, atheistic, younger generation of contemporary Soviet society. The story is static, like a painting depicting the traditional procession around the church during the Easter midnight service. Arrogant teenagers jam the churchyard to observe what seems to them an anachronism. The contrast between the religious procession and the blasphemous spectators is simply but powerfully presented.

The story is complicated, however, by one brief paragraph which introduces a third element:

> Among the believers I catch a glimpse of one or two Jewish faces. Perhaps they are converts, or perhaps they are just onlookers. Glancing around warily, they too are waiting for the Easter procession. We all curse the Jews, but it would be worthwhile having a look around us to see what kind of Russians we have bred at the same time.[28]

The Jewish observers in the churchyard apparently function as a mirror that Solzhenitsyn holds up to the nation so that Russians

will see themselves and be ashamed. The few Jews in the churchyard respect this place of worship; they do not mock it. The ordinary Russian considers the Jew far removed from the Orthodox
Church, and does not expect him to exhibit either interest in or
respect for its services. The Jews Solzhenitsyn describes, however,
are much more sympathetic to the church than the representatives
of the younger Russian generation. They may even be converts.
Thus cultural, ethnic, and religious differences may be less pronounced than the gap between generations in modern Russian
society.

The second theme Solzhenitsyn sounds in this passage embraces
one of the ugliest features of Russian life, anti-Semitism. Solzhenitsyn is not accusing all Russians of anti-Semitism, but nevertheless
he emphasizes its constant pervasiveness in the USSR. At the same
time, he questions the basis for the Russians' national pride in view
of their contempt for the defenseless Jewish minority. He typically
appeals to the conscience of the Russians as he asks what sort of
younger generation they have reared in recent years. The description of the crowd of teenagers at the beginning of the story is his
eloquent answer.

The didacticism of "The Easter Procession" is characteristic of
Solzhenitsyn's so-called "prose poems," or miniatures. They
unfailingly convey one rather simple idea and resemble Tolstoy's
didactic stories written for the Russian peasant. In sharp contrast
to Solzhenitsyn's short stories, however, his miniatures and prose
poems present little of artistic or intellectual interest.

CHAPTER 6

# *Drama*

I  *Solzhenitsyn as Playwright*

A S one of Solzhenitsyn's most important literary achievements
is his highly developed narrative style, his efforts as a playwright necessitated an enormous adjustment in craftsmanship. The
reader who can fully appreciate Solzhenitsyn's language in the
original finds his dynamic narrative, his precise and often unusual
lexicon, exceptionally persuasive. But in drama the narrator is
absent, the entire text consists of the direct speech of characters
whose language cannot deviate very substantially from the standard of a given social milieu. If Solzhenitsyn's plays fail, they do so
partly because of an inherent feature of the genre itself — the
absence of the narrator.

Solzhenitsyn's didacticism also helps account for his lack of
success in playwriting. His intensely moralistic tone is much more
acceptable in narrative prose than on the stage. As his characters
usually advocate opposing philosophies, an omniscient narrator
who analyzes their thoughts and feelings without constantly placing
them in direct confrontations can develop the personages more
convincingly. On the stage, however, Solzhenitsyn's characters
develop their philosophies through continual ideological clashes
that fail to develop into plausible dialogues, for their very intensity
lends an artificial quality to them. Still, Solzhenitsyn's two dramas
are important to this study, for they add an extra dimension to his
*Weltanschauung* and help link his artistic works with his extra-
literary statements.

At first glance his two plays, *The Love Girl and the Innocent* and
*The Candle in the Wind,* appear complementary in almost every
respect. The protagonist of each encounters an alien, hostile world
to which he acclimates himself only with difficulty. Rodion Nemov
arrives at a concentration camp from the army, and Alex Koriel

moves from camp and exile into free society — at least as free as a society can be under the strict control of a military-industrial establishment. Both men have something positive to offer their new surroundings. At this point, however, the similarities between the plays end.

*The Love Girl and the Innocent,* in a concentration camp in the USSR, exposes the reader to a world similar to that portrayed in *One Day in the Life of Ivan Denisovich. The Candle in the Wind,* on the other hand, takes place in an unspecified and imaginary but highly industrialized and scientifically advanced society. This play bears some relationship to *The First Circle* in that both examine scientific progress and the abuse of technology by the power structure in an almost anti-utopian society with a critical eye. The play parallels *The Cancer Ward* in that both illustrate the arrogance of scientists, and in that the protagonists of both are ex-convicts who face problems in readjusting to normal society.

## II   The Love Girl and the Innocent

In *The Love Girl and the Innocent,* Solzhenitsyn attempts to compensate for the absence of the narrator whom he used so successfully in *One Day in the Life of Ivan Denisovich.* The set extends from the stage into the auditorium proper. Barbed wire is stretched between the audience and the orchestra. If the audience should interfere with the changing of the camp guard during the intermissions, the author directs, an officer must shout, "Get back from the wire! Stop crowding!"[1] Similar devices, originally introduced in the Soviet Union by Vsevolod Meyerhold in the 1920's, are meant to involve the audience in the action of the play to the greatest extent possible.

The stage directions further call for a grotesque contrast between the actual brutality of the concentration camp, and the government propaganda promulgated through posters, slogans, and songs. Behind the first curtain is a second—

A length of fabric crudely painted with a poster-like industrial landscape, depicting cheerful, apple-cheeked, muscular men and women working away quite effortlessly. In one corner of the curtain a joyful procession is in progress complete with flowers, children and a portrait of Stalin.[2]

When the curtain bearing Stalin's portrait is exposed, the orchestra

plays the theme from the film *Veselye rebyata* (The Jolly Fellows),
which every Soviet associates with such verses as:

> March forward, you Komsomol race.
> Joke and sing so that smiles will flower.
> We conquer time and space.
> We young are the owners of the planet.[3]

A prisoner continues to play the tune on a harmonica after the
poster-curtain is lifted. The contrast between this idyllic scene and
the appearance of the prisoners is understandably sinister.

Unfortunately, this grotesquery does not permeate the play.
Instead, it turns into a melodrama in which only the villains resemble real people, while the positive characters lack all persuasiveness.
Nemov, who enjoys some authority in a supervisory capacity in the
camp, tries to be fair to his hard-working fellow convicts and to
stem the corruption of the privileged few who hold office, hospital,
or kitchen jobs, but his attempts are astonishingly naive, and he
soon loses his position. Having again become a lowly convict
laborer, he swiftly concludes that conscience is the most important
thing in life, a discovery he shares with Lyuba, the camp prostitute,
who falls in love with him.

*Nemov:* You know something, sometimes I think to myself, are our lives
so important? Are they the most valuable thing we have?
*Lyuba: (With great attention)* What else is there?
*Nemov:* It sounds funny talking about it here in the camp, but maybe ...
conscience ...
*Lyuba: (Gazing at him intently)* Do you think so?[4]

In *The First Circle,* Volodin reaches a similar conclusion, but he
does not express his thought so ineptly, and certainly not to a person whom he barely knows. Furthermore, Solzhenitsyn carefully
motivates the change in Volodin's philosophy. Nemov, however,
rather resembles one of the portraits on the poster-curtain as he
himself comments: "Well, look at me — chiselling off the slag,
singing songs ..."[5]

The plot is predictable: Nemov falls in love with Lyuba. The
scene in which she overwhelms him with her "professional skill" is
ludicrously clichéd.

*Nemov:* Lyubonka, what's happening to me?

*Lyuba:* What indeed? *(They kiss)*

*Nemov:* Who taught you to kiss like that?

*Lyuba:* I learnt ... *(They kiss)*

*Nemov:* Lyuba, you're ... you're a desperate woman. You seem to drink
me in, swallow me. I won't be without you now, do you hear me? I
can't be without you...

*Lyuba:* We only got to know each other today, and you say you can't live
without me?[6]

The merits of *The Love Girl and the Innocent* have never been
tested on the stage. The Moscow Sovremennik Theater accepted the
play for production in 1962, but never actually performed it. One
doubts, however, that a stage performance would do very much for
the play.

### III   The Candle In the Wind

Solzhenitsyn's second play, *The Candle in the Wind,* subtitled
"The Light Which Is in Thee," is more enjoyable reading and also
reveals his religious and philosophical views more fully. Pairs of
characters share certain obvious similarities even as they differ
markedly in temperament, in background, and, above all, in their
philosophies. Two friends, Alex and Filipp, have returned from
imprisonment to normal life: they adopt completely different lifestyles and argue vigorously over the values of their society. Filipp
views his years in prison and the labor camp as a total waste and
desperately struggles to catch up with his contemporaries, who
have not spent a decade behind barbed wire. At the time of his re-
union with Alex, Filipp is in charge of a biocybernetics department
in a university and in a position to offer Alex an attractive position.
Unlike Filipp, Alex feels that his best years spent in concentration
camp and exile were far from wasted. They may even have been the
most important period in his life for molding his character and
philosophy. After his release from the labor camp, instead of
hurrying to reassimilate himself into society, he spends five additional years in voluntary exile on the periphery of the civilized
world in order, as he puts it, to think his thoughts through to some
meaningful conclusions. Alex does not blindly accept all the values
and advantages of normal life that are available to him in a relatively free society. Rather he is critical of them. Viewing modern
civilization — its institutions, values, and everyday life — in his

new perspective, he now finds them wanting. This intellectual schism between the two main characters is reflected in their behavior. Whereas Filipp lives harmoniously in society, Alex remains an outsider. Only reluctantly at the beginning of the play does he take part in the activities prescribed by the generally accepted code of behavior.

Alex is not alone, however, in his opposition to the *status quo*. His young cousin Alda, whom he barely remembers from the time prior to his arrest, has a refined mind and superior sensitivity which ill equip her for the artificial, brutal life of an industrialized society. There is a definite link between Alex and Alda even though they differ greatly in strength and intellectual awareness. As Alex has groped his way to a new *Weltanschauung* through long and painful years in a labor camp, voluntary isolation, and intensive meditation, his rejection of the lifestyle of his society is conscious and thoroughly considered. Alda, however, though existentially in full agreement with Alex's principles, is intellectually incapable of either understanding his philosophy or formulating her own reasons for her rejection of society's values. The two cousins have arrived at the same conclusions by different routes: Alex through conscientious, intellectual effort sparked by his exceptional experience, Alda through an intuitive resentment of a primitive, brutal, and materialistic society. Alex and Alda are misfits, born losers, as they would be labeled in many communities today, while Filipp is praised as a successful and valuable member of society.

The opportunity to engage in scientific research again and the natural need of a lonely man for love and sharing are the only attractions this society has for Alex. At first his work in the biocybernetics department and his rewarding relationship with Alda seem to satisfy his needs. His happiness is short-lived, however, because he attempts to merge these two enthusiasms of his by helping the over-sensitive Alda through biocybernetics and simultaneously furthering social progress by applying the latest scientific knowledge for the benefit of man. Alda's conversion and her conviction that her troubles will end when she undergoes a special treatment for "neuro-stabilization" border on science-fiction.

The treatment, as could easily have been predicted, is simultaneously a stunning success and a total failure. Alda is transformed into an unemotional automaton who does not experience fear, anxiety, or hesitation. She is perfectly adjusted to industrialized and shallow society and shares the trivial tastes and aspirations of her contemporaries. She is happy in the sense that she is freed of spiritual conflict. Filipp considers her treatment a triumph of science and a victory for his career and his department. Alex, on the other hand, views her "neuro-stabilization" as a catastrophe, for it simply destroys all of Alda's humanity. She is transformed from a highly gifted and sensitive woman into a shadow of herself, merely a breathing organism. Alex perceives her metamorphosis as a tragedy: in his view her infantile happiness cannot justify the destruction of her personality.

Alex's disillusionment leads to the examination of another theme, scientific progress and consumerism. Having returned from labor camp and exile with a value system in which the spiritual plays the dominant role, Alex wonders seriously whether he should resume his career as a scientist. He argues with Filipp that science and industry fail to engender, and often even corrupt, precisely those values which are most important. In Alex, Solzhenitsyn pictures the despair of the intellectual who sees the world about him disintegrating but who is powerless to do anything about it, for his contemporaries either do not hear his words or do not heed them. Fearful of scientific and technological progress, Alex reluctantly resigns from the biocybernetic institute with vague plans to join an unprestigious socio-cybernetic research department in order to prevent the further abuse of knowledge. His friends abandon him; he lives in poverty and refuses to associate with anyone, for these seemingly healthy and intelligent people who waste their lives on trivia depress him. The most important characteristics of this society are its materialism, acquisitiveness, and utter· spiritual emptiness. Actually the only values that the people around Alex embrace are personal ambition, sex, greed, and pleasure.

Solzhenitsyn lends credibility to Alex's anxiety over negative technological progress which feeds materialism and acquisitiveness by introducing the power structure of this imaginary society into the play. It is difficult to decide whether it is capitalistic or socialistic, *i.e.,* on which side of the Iron Curtain it is located, but plainly it is highly industrialized and well organized under an almost omnipotent government controlled to a large extent by the military. Fittingly, a representative of the military establishment displays great interest in Alda now that "neuro-stabilization" has transformed her into a talking vegetable. He wonders whether she is completely fearless, and when she answers affirmatively, he wants to know whether "neuro-stabilization" can be used on the masses.

Apparently the defense department is toying with the idea of preparing some kind of human robots for military purposes. The next step in the dehumanizing process, as Alex sees it, is to penetrate the human mind, to discover a way to register thoughts graphically, and then to decode the graphs. Solzhenitsyn strongly emphasizes this anti-utopian aspect of scientific progress.

*The Candle in the Wind,* like *The Cancer Ward,* examines the right of scientists and technologists to assume responsibility for and authority over an individual. As Kostoglotov assaults the dehumanizing rigidity of modern medicine as an institution, so does Nemov counter the arrogance of the cyberneticists. Both protagonists end up alone, retreating from the field of struggle into a bleak future. Both the novel and the play are passionate denunciations of the dehumanization of our society in the electronic age. Solzhenitsyn apparently considers the technological threat to mankind even greater than that of totalitarianism.

## CHAPTER 7

# August 1914 *and*
# The Gulag Archipelago 1918-1956

SOLZHENITSYN'S two lengthiest works are either not yet completely published or still being written. *August 1914* begins a monumental historical trilogy, only the first part of which has appeared. *The Gulag Archipelago 1918-1956,* an immense study of the Soviet judicial and penal systems, consists of seven parts, only two of which appeared in print abroad while Solzhenitsyn was still living in the USSR. Different though the two works are, they nevertheless share certain features which justify discussing them in the same chapter: In these two works Solzhenitsyn approaches the world of the convict in Stalin's empire less as a denouncer than as an investigator of the genesis of these horrors. Nevertheless, both works are written from the dissenter's point of view. *August 1914* traces the origins of the Soviet government, *i.e.,* the history of the Russian Revolution, Lenin's seizure of power in 1917, and the subsequent establishment of the Soviet judicial and penal systems. *The Gulag Archipelago 1918-1956* deals with the question of who is really to blame for the horrors that millions of Soviet citizens, including the author, endured under Stalin.

## I   August 1914

The plot of the first part of the historic trilogy is virtually non-existent: nearly all the facts described, with the exception of General Samsonov's death, represent the first stages of individual plot lines which no doubt will be fully developed only in subsequent parts of the book.

The greatest part of the text is devoted to the military operations of the Russian Army in East Prussia, while only one-fifth of the volume deals with peaceful life in Russia itself. To the latter belong

130

the first chapters, describing the rural life of the family of Tomchak, a rich landowner of humble origin who has acquired considerable wealth. In the same part of the book a young university student, Sanya, seeks spiritual advice from Leo Tolstoy, who appears in his garden during his morning walk and says a few words to the youth.

The major events on the front line are united through the main character, General Staff Colonel Vorotyntsev, who, not being attached to any military unit, is always moving from one place to the other, trying to coordinate disorganized troops and to collect reliable information for headquarters.

*August 1914* ends with the total defeat of the Russian Second Army in East Prussia, the suicide of its Commander, General Samsonov, and a daringly critical speech by Colonel Vorotyntsev at the supreme Headquarters of the Russian Army.

Solzhenitsyn's preoccupation with historical investigation is not surprising, in view of his other works and that personal faith which led him into various camps, prisons, and exile. The historical novel *August 1914* is a prose epic depicting all strata of prerevolutionary Russia during both a time of relative peace and World War I. It is tempting to compare it with Tolstoy's *War and Peace,* but though such a comparison may be justified, Solzhenitsyn's work contains many additional features found neither in Tolstoy nor in the Russian literary tradition. The text incorporates several new literary devices along with extra-literary material, through which Solzhenitsyn creates an alloy of fiction and documentary. Under the heading "screen," cinematic passages are set off from the rest of the narrative; stage directions are indented in the text. Other devices recalling some of the techniques used by John Dos Passos reinforce the documentary nature of *August 1914,* but here their function is more esthetic than communicative. The same is true of the extra-literary material. "Documents" and "random selections from newspapers" (defined by quotation marks), as well as proverbs, poems placed at the end of certain chapters, and excerpts from folk and military songs, function aphoristically. Certain chapters designated by single quotation marks as "survey chapters" create further interrelated signs interacting with others in the main narrative. The repeated image of the turning wheel, for example, in the cinematic sections is obviously a central one, and probably will recur in the subsequent parts of the trilogy.

These elements function on a purely stylistic level as well.

Although they appear to be disconnected, they are in fact unified: they parallel the mainstream of the narrative and contribute to the interaction of various devices. When traditional means of expression (the folk song and the proverb) are interspersed with features common to such modern mass communication media as the press and the cinema (newspaper headlines, for example), time barriers begin to dissolve. The mobilization of the nation for war recalls the martial mood of ancient times, but its war machine bears the stamp of the modern age.

Solzhenitsyn's blend of ancient with modern historical perspective is essential to this novel. He seemingly accepts Tolstoy's interpretation of history as expressed in *War and Peace,* but at the same time he sets himself apart from Tolstoy's philosophy of history and, in particular, from his interpretation of war. Solzhenitsyn does not share Tolstoy's belief that an individual, no matter how great his authority, can never control large masses of people and thus impress his will on historical events. Both Solzhenitsyn and his protagonist, Colonel Vorotyntsev, consider war a complex and difficult undertaking demanding skill, technology, and initiative. Solzhenitsyn claims the Russian army lacked all three in 1914.

The decisive element in war, as in any other social or political process, in both Tolstoy and Solzhenitsyn's view, is the spirit of the masses: the nation and its army. The difference between the two authors lies in their understanding of that spirit. Tolstoy assumes that the morale of an army is only loosely related to the actions of its commanders, and that this spirit appears in some half-mysterious, irrational fashion. Solzhenitsyn, on the other hand, sees a direct link between the professional skills of officers and the morale of their troops, although, like Tolstoy, he acknowledges the decisive role played by spirit in actual combat. One may thus conclude that Solzhenitsyn adheres to the Tolstoyan tradition, but modified in accordance with the experience of his generation.

Solzhenitsyn's depiction of an old and inefficient Russian general parodies another Tolstoyan thesis. In Solzhenitsyn's view, the contrast Tolstoy builds between General Kutuzov and Napoleon, particularly during the battle of Borodino, is damaging to the Russian military spirit and to the nation as a whole. Many Russians, including certain members of the military, misinterpreted and later idealized Kutuzov's passivity in that major battle of the 1812 campaign.

In *August 1914* the mediocre General Blagoveshchensky not only mutilates Tolstoy's ideas but believes the myth which the nation, or rather its ruling class, has created to compensate for its own feelings of insecurity and anguish. The architects of official rhetoric simply borrowed several passages from Tolstoy describing the natural strength, ingenuity, and perseverance of the Russian people, combined them with his notion of the unpredictability of historical events, and created a strange concoction of superstition and chauvinistic fatalism. It goes without saying that such a mindset did not stimulate the acquisition of knowledge or the development of military skills and technology.

Solzhenitsyn is in complete agreement with Tolstoy on many points. Both condemn the bureaucracy inherent in social institutions. *August 1914* contains numerous such examples, the most obvious being the inaccurate dispatches written by General Blagoveshchensky. The tranquility that his corps enjoyed on the Prussian border was due, not to his Kutuzov-like wisdom and caution, but rather to his bureaucratic manipulations.

General Blagoveshchensky's criminal falsification of the facts in his military dispatches is an even greater threat to the Russian army than the German artillery and, in Solzhenitsyn's view, was chiefly responsible for Russia's defeat. A complex web of persistent lies is slowly woven about the chief commander, General Samsonov, a web which eventually drives him to suicide and his army to virtual annihilation. It is the lie that Solzhenitsyn fears most: he can neither justify it nor forgive it. In *The First Circle* and "An Incident at Krechetovka Station" he demonstrates the manner in which lies, destruction, and death are inextricably intertwined; but he depicts the destructiveness of the lie most powerfully in *August 1914*.

The links between *August 1914* and *War and Peace* are many. Platon Karataev, a soldier of peasant stock whom Pierre Bezukhov meets while in French captivity and whom Tolstoy presents as the epitome of the simple Russian man, finds his counterpart in Solzhenitsyn's novel in the figure of Arsenii Blagodaryov. A private also of peasant stock he deeply impresses Colonel Vorotynsev. "There was in this soldier a great fund of simple humanity — a goodness that had nothing to do with rank, class, or politics but was the unspoiled simplicity of Nature herself."[1] What Vorotyntsev values above all in Blagodaryov is the fact that he is totally unaffected by the bureaucratic machinery of society. Blagodaryov is not only close to nature, but he also enjoys an organic relationship with his country's history. He has an intuitive sense of belonging to the national tradition, almost as if all the centuries of Russia's history were his own personal biography. One of the most powerful scenes in *August 1914* describes the Russian infantry caught in German artillery fire as Blagodaryov screams into Vorotyntsev's ear "Threshing floor!" to describe the havoc the German grenades are wreaking on the Russian troops. The agricultural image of the battle harkens back to a passage in the twelfth-century Russian epic, *Slovo o polku Igoreve* (The Lay of Igor's Campaign), which depicts the strife in medieval Russia:

> On the river Nemiga they spread haystacks
>     of human heads.
> They threshed them with steel flails,
> Leaving bodies on the threshing floor.
> They winnowed the souls from their bodies.
> The bloody shores of the Nemiga River
> Were sown not with wheat.
> They were sown with the bones of Russia's sons.[2]

This image comes naturally to Blagodaryov, a simple, uneducated man. He has no notion of *The Lay of Igor's Campaign* but his perception of the horror of war is virtually identical to that of the epic's unknown author. Blagodaryov's comment implies still another connection between these two epochs, for he speaks in 1914, only four years before the beginning of the Russian Civil War, which would prove no less destructive than the feudal wars of ancient Russia.

Solzhenitsyn also emphasizes the religious propensities of the prerevolutionary Russian as a sign of his linkage with the ancient national tradition. Again, Blagodaryov is a good example of this. When the regiment commander falls on the battlefield and must be hastily interred, Blagodaryov assumes the role of priest with natural ease: "Chest out, head up, he turned to the rising sun and in a clear, strong voice, precisely in the style of an Orthodox deacon, intoned to the high pine tops: 'In peace let us pray to the Lord!'"[3]

Solzhenitsyn uses religious belief to link seemingly disparate characters. Private Blagodaryov and General Samsonov, for instance, share a genuinely religious view of the world and of historical events: before the latter commits suicide, he kneels down in the forest to pray.

At the same time that Solzhenitsyn movingly and warmly describes the sincere prayers of men engaged in combat, he depicts with caustic sarcasm the hypocritical, official religious orthodoxy, pressed into service to justify indecisiveness and lack of leadership. This contrast is most poignant in the scene between Grand Duke Nicholas, the commander-in-chief of the Russian Army, and the chaplain, when the Grand Duke seriously dreams of military success from the dispatching to the front of a wonder-working icon. At the end of the chapter Solzhenitsyn expresses his own opinion on this subject with the proverb "Praying kneads no dough."

Solzhenitsyn's accuracy in his depiction of historical events and the tenor of life in Russia during World War I will no doubt be questioned and debated. However, even if a reexamination of this fateful epoch in Russian history should be the only result of his exceptionally bold undertaking, his efforts will not have been in vain.

## II   The Gulag Archipelago

*The Gulag Archipelago 1918-1956* (Parts I and II) has already engendered heated controversy, and no doubt the debate will continue when the book's remaining five parts appear. It bears an unusual subtitle ("An Attempt at an Artistic Investigation"), and one comes to realize only later that this refers to the way the author has assembled his enormous quantity of material. His method of accumulating it was, of course, unusual because of the circumstances surrounding his work. The bulk of his information was provided by eyewitnesses to or participants in various events whom he met as a prisoner in labor camps. Because all this information was transmitted to him orally and recorded only in his memory, his investigation is, of course, unscholarly. Therefore it is appropriate to characterize it as an "artistic investigation," and thereby link it with the endeavor of an artist who gathers his material through his eyes and ears and stores it in his memory.

Solzhenitsyn's unusual method of gathering his data is reflected in the way the book is written. First, this enormous epic is a vast mosaic. Some sections are clearly autobiographical; others consist of quotations from the few available documents or reconstructions of testimony given by eyewitnesses; still others are precise renderings of specific personal accounts passed on to Solzhenitsyn by participants in the events. This very diversity of narrative techniques stylistically relates *The Gulag Archipelago* more closely to *August 1914* than to any of Solzhenitsyn's other works.

The unusual means by which Solzhenitsyn gathered his material for *The Gulag Archipelago* dictated the very personal form of his account. Indeed, without the unifying thread provided by the author's voice, the diverse materials would be too loosely organized to form a coherent narrative. Solzhenitsyn expresses his feelings most effectively through intonation. There are passages in which one cannot avoid hearing his outraged cry. Sometimes he resorts to sarcasm or irony; at certain points he lapses into profound sorrow. In many ways he himself is the hero of *The Gulag Archipelago:* it lacks a protagonist, and the narrator's omniscience and his emotions make one unnecessary. The narrative style alone transforms the book from a document into the "artistic investigation" that Solzhenitsyn planned.

*The Gulag Archipelago* must be regarded not only as the major modern indictment by a single citizen of his country's major modern totalitarian government, but also as an unparalleled act of courage and heroism. At the very least, the average reader must experience a sense of bewilderment after reading the first two parts of *The Gulag Archipelago*. As George Kennan put it in his brilliant review of the book,

> The initial reaction to Mr. Solzhenitsyn's account is less indignation against the authors of these horrors and injustices, though of course there is that, too, than discouragement, great sadness, and no small measure of puzzlement over the fact that such things could have taken place in our own time in a country sharing the Christian tradition, a country that has been the source of some of the greatest literature, and the greatest moral teaching of the modern age, a country with which we were in effect allied during the recent war, and with which we fancied ourselves to have in common at least certain standards of decency and humanity that would set us off against our common enemy.[4]

It is virtually impossible to pinpoint the single most devastating incident in the book, for the entire work is a series of horrors, each worse than the one preceding it. Those familiar with Solzhenitsyn's other works will not be surprised by the gloomy atmosphere of *The Gulag Archipelago*. Yet his description of the activity of the OSO (Special Commission of the MGB), an institution empowered with vast judicial authority but functioning exclusively within the administrative branch of the government, is surely one of his most shocking revelations. This special commission has codified its own criminal law, containing the following eleven articles of indictment, each designated by a Russian acronym.

| | |
|---|---|
| ASA | — Anti-Soviet Agitation |
| KRD | — Counter-Revolutionary Activity |
| KRTD | — Counter-Revolutionary Trotskyite Activity (This letter "T" made the life of a *zek* much harder in the labor camps.) |
| PSh | — Suspicion of Espionage (Espionage substantiated by more than mere suspicion was referred to a tribunal.) |
| SVPSh | — Contacts leading (!) to Suspicion of Espionage |
| KRM | — Counter-Revolutionary Thought |
| VAS | — Nurturing Anti-Soviet Feelings |
| SOE | — Socially Dangerous Elements |
| SVE | — Socially Harmful Elements |
| PD | — Criminal Activity (readily imputed to an ex-convict if there was nothing else of which to accuse him) |

And finally, there was the comprehensive article:

| | |
|---|---|
| ChS | — Member of the Family (of a person convicted under any of the above articles).[5] |

Clearly any citizen could be accused under one of these articles, the most commonly used being SVPSh, KRM, or VAS. These last two articles actually allow the authorities to persecute a man solely for his thoughts and feelings. Such articles as PSh, SVPSh, and ChS also cover potential crimes.

One of the major points of *The Gulag Archipelago* is that Stalin's role in creating this infernal system of governmental terror should not be exaggerated. By no means does Solzhenitsyn attempt to diminish Stalin's responsibility; the author simply names others who share the blame for the government's criminal acts. The first two parts of *The Gulag Archipelago* make it clear that Solzhenitsyn considers Lenin the actual creator of the Soviet penal system and argues that Stalin only perfected and perpetuated it. *The Gulag Archipelago* — this hidden side of the USSR, this unknown land with its population, culture, hierarchy, and language, the land of the *zeks* such as Ivan Denisovich and Nerzhin — is in Solzhenitsyn's opinion not the product of a single man, but rather of the political system established after the revolution of 1917 and proclaimed by Lenin the dictatorship of the proletariat. The system operates, not according to law, but by exterminating its political and social enemies. How cruel and ruthless this extermination was Solzhenitsyn has richly documented in *The Gulag Archipelago*. But even more astonishing is the incredible stupidity of this self-defeating system. Renowned specialists in all fields become victims of the Cheka, GPU, NKVD, MGB, KGB, *et al.* — all abbreviations for the Soviet secret police at various times. How a nation could exist, develop industrially, win a war with Germany, even outlive the immortal Stalin, launch the first Earth satellite, and go on to challenge the greatest powers of the world under the conditions Solzhenitsyn exposes remains an enigma. An even greater mystery is how those individuals Solzhenitsyn portrays could possibly remain uncowed, idealistic, and heroic in this environment.

## CHAPTER 8

# Craftsman and Thinker

I *Solzhenitsyn and the Russian Language*

IMMEDIATELY upon the publication of Solzhenitsyn's first book, his readers and critics recognized two vital characteristics of his art — his language, and his straightforward depiction of the inhumanity of Stalin's labor camps. Solzhenitsyn's Russian readers appreciated the innovative form and content of his fiction from his initial appearance on the literary scene. His style — which contrasts sharply with the bleak, stereotyped language of contemporary Soviet fiction — is based upon the Russian vernacular, flavored with the jargon of the labor camp and with archaic, long-forgotten word formations. The latter are often so surprising and refreshing that one might think Solzhenitsyn had invented his own neologisms. Actually, he has for the most part merely restored the beauty and richness of the Russian language, which entered a decline after the revolution of 1917.

The idiosyncracies of Solzhenitsyn's style blend organically with the content of his various works. His use of the vernacular and the jargon of the labor camp enables him to create in *One Day in the Life of Ivan Denisovich* a very effective *skaz,* oral narration, that adds credibility to the story and contributes to its powerful effect upon the reader. The oral character of Solzhenitsyn's narration, coupled with his use of archaic word formations, makes his prose unusually dynamic; and the exceptionally rich content of his lexicon lends additional nuances to the text.[1] By concentrating a large amount of information within relatively brief passages, Solzhenitsyn engenders a rapid flow of ideas and images which create the impression of a totally spontaneous, improvised account. This apparent spontaneity of Solzhenitsyn's narrative makes his works unusually convincing and powerful.

Solzhenitsyn's language also serves to distinguish his prose stylistically from standardized contemporary Soviet literature and the

139

mass media, and thus to bridge the "credibility gap," if one may apply this term to the distrust of the average Soviet citizen for the printed word in his country. The press and the literati have for so long abused the language with clichés of official rhetoric that its effect upon the reader has been reduced to a minimum. Solzhenitsyn's immediate success may to a large extent have been due to his new and fresh use of language.

## II  *Solzhenitsyn and Dostoevsky*

In his fiction Solzhenitsyn effectively employs a technique called "polyphony," a device originally detected in Dostoevsky's works by Mikhail Bakhtin, a leading Russian literary scholar of the Formalist school. With only slight modification, Solzhenitsyn incorporates this device into his novels: almost every one of his characters shares in the development of the theme as if he were the book's protagonist. In any given passage the narrator focuses exclusively on a particular character. The effect is one of intense interaction among a multitude of independent and seemingly unrelated characters, or "polyphony." Only a tight structure can unify them within the framework of a novel or short story.

Ironically, Solzhenitsyn's characters act independently in just those circumstances that would seem to offer little possibility of individual freedom. Within the confines of a concentration camp or a hospital, freedom of action is, to say the least, limited. Yet while constraining his characters physically, Solzhenitsyn expands their intellectual independence and spiritual freedom. The reader thus witnesses the paradoxical depiction of free men in chains. From the grey mass of convicts and hospital patients emerge bright and colorful individuals, each with his unique outlook and destiny. The contrast between the author's portrayal of individual personalities and the bureaucratic equation of a man with a number or a medical chart eloquently conveys Solzhenitsyn's humanism.

The strict temporal and spatial limits of Dostoevsky's works — usually set within the confines of one town or city — are also characteristic of Solzhenitsyn's fiction, which reduces the world to a concentration camp, a hospital, a small village, or a railroad station. The limits expand somewhat in *The First Circle,* for here only some of the characters are actually imprisoned, and the remainder live in Moscow; yet all are subjected to strict spatial limitations, as Stalin's prison-like office strikingly demonstrates.

With the exception of Yakonov, who strolls nightly in Moscow, and Volodin, who calls a doctor from a telephone booth, the characters other than convicts are shown for the most part in their offices or apartments.

Time in Solzhenitsyn's novels, likewise, is extremely condensed. His Dostoevskian concentration of a great many events within a brief span strengthens the depiction of the characters' inner freedom. Though they are deprived of their liberty, their lives still appear rich and meaningful because of the concentration of a wide range of emotional states and intellectual endeavors within a short period of time. The tightness of space and time reinforces the polyphonic presentation of the characters in such a way that each appears intellectually free and independent. This kind of presentation requires a certain distance between the narrator and his characters: the latter's independence is directly proportional to their distance from the former. Although Solzhenitsyn's style is highly personal, his narrators' emotional involvement with the events they describe is slight (although this is generally so, it is less true of "Matryona's House," with its first-person narrator, and *The Gulag Archipelago 1918-1956,* which stands apart from Solzhenitsyn's other works). The narrator's distance is surprising in view of the fact that suffering — physical pain, mental anguish, and fear of death — plays a major part in Solzhenitsyn's works. Suffering is more central to *The Cancer Ward,* in which the narrator stands closer to the characters, than in the novel about prison life. In the latter, the narrator's aloofness suggests the cruel indifference to human suffering that prevails in the convict's world. The lack of compassion in all these works is striking, and distinguishes Solzhenitsyn's fiction radically from Dostoevsky's in its emotional impact. Though these two authors structure their works and handle space and time similarly, that compassion for one's fellow human beings so basic and essential to Dostoevsky, seems lacking in Solzhenitsyn. At the risk of oversimplification, one may say that for Dostoevsky a human being is essentially a person with the capacity for compassion, whereas for Solzhenitsyn a human being is primarily a person dedicated to the truth and capable of defending his own dignity.[2]

## III  *Solzhenitsyn and Tolstoy*

Solzhenitsyn's preoccupation with the question of human sur-

vival, coupled with his own personal experience, no doubt caused
him to bring his characters into a direct confrontation with death.
In order to create a more persuasive picture of deadly danger, he
periodically employs an artistic device which Victor Shklovsky
termed "defamiliarization" (*ostranenie*). Frequently found in
Tolstoy's works, it is defined as the presentation of a familiar
object or action from a distance in such a way that the reader must
exert additional effort to recognize and identify it; consequently it
impresses one more deeply than would the customary presentation.
Solzhenitsyn uses this device in *The Cancer Ward* to communicate
the grave danger of the intensive X-ray treatment:

Through the square of skin that had been left clear on his stomach,
through the layers of flesh and organs whose names their owner himself
did not know, through the mass of the toadlike tumor, through the stomach and entrails, through the blood that flowed along his arteries and
veins, through lymph and cells, through the spine and lesser bones and
again through more layers of flesh, vessels and skin on his back, then
through the hard wooden board of the couch, through the four-
centimeter-thick floorboards, through the props, through the filling
beneath the boards, down, down, until they disappeared into the very
stone foundations of the building or into the earth, poured the harsh X
rays, the trembling vectors of electric and magnetic fields, unimaginable to
the human mind, or else the more comprehensible quanta that like shells
out of guns pounded and riddled everything in their path.[3]

The enumeration of objects bombarded by the X-rays — wood,
stone, and finally the earth itself, which cannot resist penetration
— shocks the reader into a realization of how deadly these rays are.
And it is essential that he comprehend their enormous power, since
their destructiveness must be weighed against their benefits
throughout the novel.

Using this same device of defamiliarization, Solzhenitsyn
describes the slow disintegration of the human organism and the
patients' torment in such excruciating detail that the reader almost
feels the pain himself:

So for no good reason at all, Yefrem had to get out of bed. He had to pass
on the will to stand to all 210 pounds of his body, the will to tense his legs,
his arms and his back, to force his flesh-laden bones out of the torpor into
which they'd begun to sink, to make their joints work and lever their bulk
upright, to become a pillar, to robe that pillar in a jacket and shift it along

corridors and down a staircase to be uselessly tormented, to have dozens of meters of bandage unwound and replaced. . .[4]

Man's confrontation with death is as essential in Solzhenitsyn's works as it is in Tolstoy's. Solzhenitsyn's description of Podduyev, who is near death, recalls Tolstoy's portrayal of Prince Andrey at the point of death in *War and Peace.* Tolstoy perceives death, not as a momentary event in a man's life, but as protracted, overlapping with life, and for a brief time almost inseparable from it. During the crisis of his illness, Prince Andrey dreams that death has entered his room despite his resistance. He then awakens and reflects on his dream:

"Yes, it was Death. I am dead, — I am awake. Yes, death is awakening," and his soul was suddenly illuminated, and the curtain which heretofore had hidden the unknown from him was raised before his mental vision. He felt, as it were, the liberation of a power that had held him fast, and that peculiar ease, which after that never left him again.[5]

Both Tolstoy and Solzhenitsyn see man as freed from the burden of life when the message of death reaches him. In *August 1914,* General Samsonov also learns of his approaching death in a dream, which he remembers after awakening:

It was altogether incomprehensible. Straining to understand, Samsonov woke up with the effort.

With the curtains undrawn, it was already light in the room, and with the light the meaning of what he had heard came clear. "Assumen" . . . the word came from "Assumption," the term the Church used for the death of the Virgin Mary. Therefore it meant: "Thou shalt die."[6]

Prince Andrey and General Samsonov alter their vision of the world radically once they know that death is imminent: they then exhibit greater spiritual awareness and drastically changed values.

A simple man in *The Cancer Ward,* Podduyev, arrives at a similar realization as he approaches death:

Pain was shooting from his neck right into his head, ceaselessly. It had started to throb evenly, in four-beat time, and each beat of the bar was hammering out: "Yefrem — Podduyev — Dead — Stop. Yefrem — Podduyev — Dead — Stop."

There was no end to it. He began to repeat words to himself, and the more he repeated them, the more remote he felt from the Yefrem Podduyev who was condemned to die. He was getting used to the idea of his own death, as one does to the death of a neighbor. But whatever it was inside him that thought of Yefrem Podduyev's death as of a neighbor's — this, it seemed, ought not to die.[7]

## IV   *Man's Heroic Resistance*

Solzhenitsyn's perception of the world is a profoundly Christian one, with definite eschatological overtones. Any nonmarxist observer can easily find events in Russian history which may be interpreted eschatologically. Many long-standing traditions and institutions have been destroyed in twentieth-century Russia. Far more destructive than the revolution of 1917 was the civil war of 1818-21, during which great numbers of the educated class left their homeland or perished. Equally important were Stalin's destruction and replacement of the Party mechanism with a new type of man and new principles of government. Even more critical were Stalin's radical, totalitarian reshaping of the country and his collectivization of agriculture in the 1930's, a move that eradicated entire social classes along with their customs, traditions, and lifestyles. The evacuation of the Crimean Tatars from the territories they had inhabited for centuries was a further step in this direction. That Solzhenitsyn should perceive history, and Russian history in particular, as an eschatological process leading to inevitable destruction (whether total or partial is irrelevant at this point) is thus not surprising. Moreover, as early as the 1920's in Paris the Russian philosopher Nicholas Berdyaev interpreted Russian history in religious terms as far back as the reforms of Peter the Great, and Solzhenitsyn doubtless was acquainted with at least some of Berdyaev's works.

Kuzyomin's code and Shukhov's discussion of God with Alyoshka, the Baptist, in *One Day in the Life of Ivan Denisovich* both suggest that the novel's protagonist is not Shukhov alone, but rather an entire nation which is forced to live by the law of the jungle. Kuzyomin's code of conduct for a labor camp and Shukhov's comments on traditional Christian teachings are as applicable to society as a whole as they are to the *zeks*. Only those with spiritual strength can survive, and they do not require the promise of future reward or the threat of punishment in the hereafter. The absolute distinction between good and evil that the Church traditionally preached would be made after the Second

Coming and the Last Judgment has in Solzhenitsyn's view already occurred in the Stalinist labor camps. According to Kuzyomin's code, the Last Judgment is here and now.

In *The Cancer Ward* Kostoglotov's equation of cancer with the ills of the political system likewise imparts a historical dimension to the personal tragedies of each character. Just as Podduyev and Rusanov must be spiritually prepared for death, so must the entire nation and all mankind recognize the transience of their existence. This undercurrent is also implicit in the very title of the anti-utopian novel *The First Circle*.

Although Solzhenitsyn's narrators are aloof and his characters in general are not preoccupied with compassion, there are times when the prisoners empathize with one another. By describing Shukhov's sympathy for Fetyukov — the least admirable member of the brigade, and one whose behavior radically contrasts with that prescribed by Kuzyomin — the narrator imbues the simple Shukhov with this special and ennobling human quality. Two of the main characters in *The First Circle* — Nerzhin and Rubin — display similar compassion for each other. Their final, moving conversation jars against the brutality of prison life:

Nerzhin's eyes, which had burned with morbid excitement during all the preparations, had now become dull and lethargic.

"Listen, friend," he said, "for three years we haven't agreed once, we've argued all the time, ridiculed each other, but now that I'm losing you, maybe forever, I feel so strongly that you are one of my most — most—"

His voice broke.

Rubin's big black eyes, so often sparkling with anger, were warm with tenderness and shyness.

"So that's all in the past," he nodded. "Let's kiss, beast."

And he took Nerzhin's face into his black pirate's beard.[8]

No analysis of Rubin's highly controversial character can afford to overlook this profound sympathy of his for Nerzhin.

It is conscience rather than compassion, however, that rests at the heart of Solzhenitsyn's works. Conscience as the last spiritual resource of a society governed by a completely materialistic philosophy is one of Solzhenitsyn's central concepts; it provides the sole motivation for heroism. Solzhenitsyn expresses this idea when he adds to the cliché "You have only one life," the phrase "and also one conscience," thus implying that conscience is as precious as life. If conditions force one to choose between the two, one must choose conscience, not life. This simple precept leads Volodin to his decision to warn an innocent doctor about a trap; it impels Gerasimovich to reject a proposal to collaborate with the authorities in *The First Circle.* Alex from *The Candle in the Wind* clearly formulates the same idea, and Kuzyomin's third commandment has two functions. In an atheistic police state, individual conscience can define an ethical standard. At the same time, conscience allows an individual faced with the dehumanizing demands of the power structure to assert his freedom. The last part of Kuzyomin's code — on informers — formulates the first function, and Volodin illustrates the second when he thinks about the risk of warning the doctor: "If one is forever cautious, can one remain a human being?"[9] Solzhenitsyn considers conscience — like the sex drive, a sense of adventure, or a sense of humor — to be a natural and inherent human trait.

Humor in Solzhenitsyn's novels occurs infrequently. When it does appear, it usually functions as a safety valve. Rubin's brilliant satire on the Soviet judicial system, when he reenacts a typical trial of a Red Army soldier who has escaped from a prisoner-of-war camp to return home, provides comic relief in *The First Circle,* with the anachronistic placing of the trial in the twelfth century and a parody of Prince Igor's return to his principality from Polovtsian captivity forming the basis of the satire. In a hilarious performance, Rubin amuses his fellow prisoners by his ridicule of Soviet justice, and provides them at least a momentary emotional release.

Those indestructible traits that make a human being capable of at least partially resisting the pressure of a modern police state are clearly essential to survival in Stalin's empire as Solzhenitsyn depicts it. Solzhenitsyn's women characters (they play less important roles because of the settings of the novels, in most instances) possess those qualities that are beyond the power of the state to control. It is no accident that the state prosecutor's daughter, Clara Makarygin, undergoes a spiritual transformation after witnessing a convict's suffering and humiliation. The sympathy that female characters display for the innocently persecuted seems in Solzhenitsyn's view to be the key to the emancipation of society. The instinctive giving of themselves by certain women independently of their upbringing and education is to some extent related to their maternal nature, at least as Solzhenitsyn sees it.

A remarkable number of Solzhenitsyn's women (Matryona in "Matryona's House": Agniya, Yakonov's fiancée seen only in a flashback, and Clara from *The First Circle;* Alda, the heroine of *The Candle in the Wind;* and to a certain degree Vega in *The Cancer Ward*) are by nature incapable of adjusting to modern, industrialized, totalitarian society. These women, who are very much alike, are almost abstractions or ideals, and yet possess a certain credibility. Their innate purity makes them superior to their male counterparts, particularly Agniya to Yakonov, Vega to Kostoglotov, Clara to Doronin, Matryona to her ex-fiancé, Faddey,[10] and in a way, to Ignatich, the story's narrator. The superiority of these women, especially to those men with whom they enter a close relationship, involves a measure of maternal feeling. This surfaces in the relationships between Agniya and Yakonov, Clara and Doronin, and Vega and Kostoglotov; it is less evident in the case of Matryona and Ignatich. The relationships between men and women in Solzhenitsyn's works thus shift significantly from erotic attraction or the professional and Party associations typical of Soviet fiction to a base of broader, mutual understanding between the sexes. Solzhenitsyn's male characters appear less aggressive, self-reliant, and dynamic as they take on the role of sufferers in need of help which only a woman can provide. It is noteworthy that in Solzhenitsyn's fiction men usually look to women to provide emotional support, and not the reverse. Moreover, with such rare exceptions such as the camp whore in *The Love-Girl and the Innocent,* sexually appealing women appear infrequently in Solzhenitsyn's works.

If the maternal instinct motivates Solzhenitsyn's female characters, an innate, indestructible, and fervent desire to know the truth drives their male counterparts. Nerzhin, who is willing to leave the relative comfort of Sharashka and descend to a lower circle of the inferno in order to preserve his freedom of thought and to continue his reflections on the destiny of his nation, is a prime example of this. In *The Candle in the Wind,* the hero Alex has remained in solitary exile for five extra years solely to clarify for himself those political and philosophical problems which have turned out to be more important to him than returning to a free life in a city. Rubin is the same kind of man, although his insatiable desire for knowledge and intellectual challenge is distorted by tragic ideological inconsistencies. The young boy Dyomka, Kostoglotov, and especially Shulubin in *The Cancer Ward* manifest the same urge:

Then Oleg asked him, "Tell me, did you think of this during those twenty-five years, while you were bowing low and renouncing your beliefs?"

Shulubin replied, his voice empty and flat, growing weaker and weaker, "Yes, I did. I renounced everything, and I went on thinking. I stuffed the old books into the stove and I turned things over in my mind. Why not? Haven't I earned the right to a few thoughts through my suffering, through my betrayal?"[11]

In a police state, man's resources for preserving his identity are reduced to the most inalienable human characteristics — conscience, intellect, maternal feeling, humor, love, adventurousness, and even sheer stubbornness. Solzhenitsyn may value them for the very reason that they do not derive from education or upbringing, which are controlled for the most part by the state, but rather are innate. Solzhenitsyn seems to believe that man is endowed with a natural and indestructible self-defense mechanism against totalitarian power, whether political or technological.

It becomes increasingly easy to see why Solzhenitsyn stresses so heavily those most fundamental human traits that may aid in resisting the overwhelming power of an atheistic police state. Humanistic principles and laws, the heritage of Western, Judeo-Christian civilization, are no longer inspiration or refuge. The individual stands alone in his quest for spiritual identity; his own weapon is personal heroism. In view of the cataclysmic events of twentieth-century Russia, the notion of heroism in Solzhenitsyn's works takes on added dimensions:

Our capacity for heroic deeds, i.e., for an extraordinary act by a single individual, is only partially a matter of will power, partially given or not given to us at birth. Most difficult for us is the heroic deed achieved through an effort of the unprepared will. It is easier if it comes from many years of long, consistent effort. And with blessed ease the heroic deed comes to us if it is as natural and simple as breathing.[12]

Thus in Solzhenitsyn's model of society only the basic human instincts, conscience, and a capacity for heroism rise in opposition to the entire administrative, technological and intellectual resources of the nation mobilized by Stalin in his struggle for total control over every single citizen.

## V   *The Structure of Solzhenitsyn's Works*

Any discussion of the structure of Solzhenitsyn's works must necessarily limit itself to his completed novels and stories, while excluding *August 1914* and *The Gulag Archipelago 1918-1956.* Solzhenitsyn organizes all of his novels and short stories with the tight precision of a mathematician. Frequently one central idea serves as the backbone of an entire work. The duality in Shukhov's personality — the perpetual conflict between his instincts and the wisdom of Kuzyomin's code — serves as the axis of *One Day in the Life of Ivan Denisovich.* In *The Cancer Ward,* Tolstoy's question "What do men live by?" establishes the central theme and is the structural device linking all the characters circumstantially assembled in the hospital. *The First Circle,* which embraces virtually all strata of Soviet society, may appear structurally more complex. The axis of this novel is a two-way spiral: the channel bearing Stalin's will from his office down to the lowest echelons of society; and the channel from there back up to the dictator, a channel which in effect negates that will.

One may argue that Solzhenitsyn's novels are structurally too schematic. This point might carry some weight had not Solzhenitsyn so skillfully covered the compositional lines of each of his works with rich and colorful details which conceal its framework. Furthermore, the structure of his novels provides the key to their interpretation and thus plays an important part in the development of his philosophy, for his major themes may be defined in large measure through an analysis of the interrelationship of various signs in the texts.

Solzhenitsyn through his works utilizes two basic types of signs — those of suppression and those of resistance — to characterize Soviet society. The most obvious signs of direct suppression are those associated with the punitive system in the USSR, most especially the concentration camps and prisons. To this group of signs belong the three basic themes of *One Day in the Life of Ivan Denisovich* — starvation, labor, and the authorities — that have already been analyzed in this study. Usually the signs of resistance are dual; one is obvious, the other much less apparent. Shukhov's stealing a few extra bowls of gruel for his brigade, for example, is an obvious sign of resistance, while the psychological implications of his elaborate eating ritual are a more subtle sign of his battle against starvation. The theme of labor also illustrates the duality of this sign system. The high work quotas and the low rating of the prisoners' daily production represent the pressure, but the convicts' resistance is two-fold: open cheating, such as Shukhov's lackadaisical scrubbing of the floor in the guards' room, and the foreman's undercover bribery of the authorities. As for the authorities themselves, the incident of the Captain's protest represents open, suicidal resistance to them, while Shukhov's stealing construction material on the worksite and then threatening the supervisor, Der, constitutes covert but quite effective resistance.

Resistance and suppression signs are consistently paired. In *The Cancer Ward* Rusanov's arrogance when he arrives at the hospital is a suppression sign opposed by Doctor Dontsova's disregard of his threats, and the imposition of hormone therapy on Kostoglotov is countered by his protests and his secret arrangement with the intern, Zoya, to avoid treatment. The sequence of these signs is most significant in *The First Circle*. Volodin's fear of warning his former family doctor is a sign of suppression; then his telephoning the physician is an act of resistance. This is followed by a suppression sign, the Sharashka convict's identification of Volodin's recorded voice which leads to the indiscriminate arrests of suspects. While the description of Sharashka obviously functions as a sign of suppression, the six confrontations in Yakonov's and Abakumov's offices are signs of resistance. Finally the theme of capital punishment, gradually reduced to the simple concept of murder, is obviously a suppression sign.

In the short stories and dramas the suppression signs are less evident, but they are present in "The Right Hand" and to some extent in "Matryona's House" and "An Incident at Krechetovka Station." Although Solzhenitsyn's play *The Love-Girl and the Innocent* does little more than duplicate almost the same sign system as that found in *One Day in the Life of Ivan Denisovich,* his second play, *The Candle in the Wind,* introduces a new sign — the military-industrial establishment, which is most effectively resisted by a refusal to participate in scientific work in this anti-utopian society, even though this leads to ostracism and poverty.

These signs of direct suppression are augmented by other sign systems, less conspicuous but perhaps more important to the critical reader, as, for example, the basic coordinates of space and time. As we have seen, space in Solzhenitsyn's works is radically restricted for the most part and so helps in creating an oppressive atmosphere. Time, however, has a double function. On the one hand, it finds expression in the long sentences the convicts are serving in concentration camps or in exile. The linkage of the protraction of time and the contraction of space engenders the complete and almost hopeless subjugation of the prisoners. Yet, on the other hand, the rich intellectual and emotional life of certain inmates endows short periods of time with significance and breaks the monotony of long terms spent in limited prison space. Imprisonment is only physical, for the inner freedom of the convicts remains intact.

A dualistic sign system is likewise characteristic of sexual differences in Solzhenitsyn's works. Solzhenitsyn's female characters are never oppressors or seekers of power. The worlds of his male and female characters are radically different. While violence and suppression characterize the men, the women are entirely oppressed and almost totally immersed in their passive but extremely tenacious struggle for freedom, both for themselves and their male counterparts. The only exception to this is Tilia, the musician's wife in *The Candle in the Wind.* One should not forget, however, that this drama does not depict the USSR exclusively. On the territory of the USSR even such female characters as Rusanov's and Makarygin's wives (both members of the privileged class) see their major role as that of caring for their children and husbands.

Solzhenitsyn's female characters are sensitive to human suffering and overleap social barriers rather easily, although always to their practical disadvantage. One recalls Clara Makarygin and Simochka, both emotionally attached to prisoners; Dr. Gangart and Zoya, both involved with Kostoglotov; and Agniya, who joins the persecuted church. Only Agniya actually falls in the social scale, but the fact that these women would even consider striking misalliances demonstrates their remarkable independence. Whether or not Solzhenitsyn idealizes women is not important; what is important is that in his totalitarian model of the world the two sexes play totally different roles. The male characters behave authoritatively towards their female counterparts even when suppressed, while the women introduce much more humanity into their relationships.

The signs of cognition, alternately suppressing and emancipating, comprise a fourth dualistic system. Solzhenitsyn depicts the suppression of truth and knowledge as the government controls all information and continually inundates the country with newly manufactured propaganda. In *The Cancer Ward,* Shulubin, a college librarian, describes the suppressive activity of the government when he recalls being forced to withdraw from circulation and destroy great numbers of books considered harmful by the authorities. Another example of suppression is the depiction of the creative process of the prominent Soviet writer Galakhov in *The First Circle.* Galakhov's self-censorship actually has the same effect as the burning of undesirable books, with the important difference that in this case the author himself destroys the truth before it even appears in the form of a manuscript. These two examples illustrate the complete expunging of the old as well as the new nonconformist ideas by Stalin's totalitarian regime.

The second instance of Stalin's attempt to control the human mind in the USSR is the huge outpouring of propaganda illustrated in *The first Circle* by the dictator's grotesque contemplation of new editions of his biography and by the description of his hyperbolic glorification throughout the country by all possible means. Solzhenitsyn introduces this type of cognitive sign obliquely throughout his works, and directly in his portrait of Stalin, from whom endlessly stream misinformation, blatant lies, and brutal indoctrination. Other examples are the brainwashing in the schools described by Asya, and the platitudes exchanged by Rusanov and his daughter in *The Cancer Ward.* The cognition-suppressing signs are also apparent in Shukhov's comments in *One Day in the Life of Ivan Denisovich* on the USSR's lack of preparation for World War II despite all the government's constant assurances that the war would be fought on foreign soil. Lieutenant Zotov ("An Incident at Krechetovka Station") perhaps best typifies the human being almost completely brainwashed by Stalin. Solzhenitsyn describes a direct indoctrination session for the Sharashka personnel in a chapter omitted from the published version of *The First Circle.*[13]

This stream of misinformation is countered by a different type of knowledge and ideas that only trickle into the lives of the characters, but still become the most significant signs in Solzhenitsyn's works. These emancipating signs counter the official lies and lead to unconventional ideas. Kuzyomin's code and a handwritten fragment from the New Testament concealed by Alyoshka the Baptist in *One Day in the Life of Ivan Denisovich* exemplify this group of signs. In the same novel the magnificent iconographic portrait of the old prisoner Y-81 also conveys a subtle message.

In *The Cancer Ward,* Tolstoy's short story "What Men Live By" serves the same structural function as Kuzyomin's code. Doctor Gangart — whose nickname, Vega, suggests her lonely, detached existence — offers Kostoglotov a new, positive view that could not possibly be openly proclaimed in the USSR with its dominant materialistic philosophy. Shulubin, again a man totally alienated from society and a representative of the pre-Stalinist period, speaks up after three decades of silence and candidly reveals his political philosophy and ideals to Kostoglotov (paralleling Shulubin is the old doctor, Oreshchenkov, who talks to Doctor Dontsova of the dehumanization of medical science under the Stalinist regime). Frosya talks quietly about God to Dyomka, who transmits his credo to Kostoglotov: "Truth is what I love." Messages reach Kostoglotov even in the zoo: the inscription on the empty monkey's cage testifying to pointless human cruelty.

In *The First Circle,* the novel in which Stalinist indoctrination is most thoroughly depicted, signs of nonconformity figure very prominently. The letters from Volodin's mother recalling the long-forgotten philosophical and cultural climate of prerevolutionary Russia trigger a spiritual metamorphosis in her son and galvanize him into following his new *Weltanschauung* boldly by warning the doctor, also a remnant of a vanished epoch. Thus Volodin subscribes to and follows the philosophy of another generation, one departed from the scene. A convict woman's accusing glance engenders a similar metamorphosis in Clara; and as the letters of Volodin's mother inspired him, he in turn enlightens his sister-in-law. Agniya, who, like Clara, is a person of independent intellect, warns Yakonov. Bobynin and Prianchikov deliver brilliant lectures to Abakumov, though in vain. In Sharashka, Spiridon answers Nerzhin's painful question about the justification of violence, and the convict artist Kondrashov-Ivanov expresses his philosophy on canvas in the image of Parsifal catching sight of the castle of the Holy Grail for the first time.

Emancipating cognitive signs in the short stories include Kordubailo's argument in "An Incident at Krechetovka Station" that might have enlightened Zotov if he had not been so indoctrinated, and the portrait of Matryona that increases the narrator's awareness in "Matryona's House."

## VI  *Interrelation of Characters*

To a certain extent Solzhenitsyn's characters fall into two categories: those who seek ideas to counter suppression, and those who offer them. The relationship between these two kinds of characters is that of donor and recipient. The recipients of emancipating ideas are invariably the protagonists, or other major characters. It is Shukhov — actually the only character in *One Day in the Life of*

*Ivan Denisovich* presented in depth — who acts upon the information received from Kuzyomin (Shukhov may pass Kuzyomin's principle along to Gopchik, but he does so through personal example rather than verbally.) In *The Cancer Ward,* Podduyev gains a new perspective on life from reading Tolstoy's story; Dontsova is privy to Oreshchenkov's thoughts about the medical profession; and Kostoglotov received vitally important concepts from Shulubin and Vega. All the recipients of wisdom stand in the foreground of the novel. In *The First Circle* the recipients are Volodin, Nerzhin, Yakonov, and Klara, all of whom are fully drawn. The same is true of the recipients in the short stories. Lieutenant Zotov and Ignatich stand in the foreground, and Mikheich, the principal in "For the Good of the Cause" who begins to understand the nature of events after his final confrontation with Khabalygin, is certainly the story's most fully realized character.

The donors, most of whom remain in the background, are a radically different group. Those on whom Solzhenitsyn focuses at all belong, not to the epoch or the society depicted, but rather to some other period or social stratum. This kind of character may be traced throughout all Solzhenitsyn's works from the beginning. Kuzyomin, intrpduced in a flashback, appears only once from a great distance, communicates his message, and disappears. He is almost as distant as Christ, about whom Alyoshka the Baptist reads in his concealed, handwritten fragment from the New Testament. Prisoner Y-81 resembles an icon or fresco seen from a distance in a church. One learns very little about Kuzyomin and Y-81; but still their impact, especially the former's, is central to the novel.

The voices of three women — Agniya and Volodin's mother in *The First Circle* and Vega in *The Cancer Ward* — also reach the reader from a distance. The first two are from the past, represent a vanished epoch, and appear in flashbacks, as does Kuzyomin; yet the impact of Volodin's mother on her son's life is as pronounced as that of Kuzyomin on the life of Ivan Denisovich. Tolstoy's message, likewise, comes from the distant past to Podduyev in *The Cancer Ward.* Solzhenitsyn obviously introduces Rusanov's grotesque confusion of Leo Tolstoy (1828–1910) with the prominent Soviet writer A.N. Tolstoy (1883–1945) in order to point up the alienation of contemporary Soviet society from Leo Tolstoy's ideas. Vega, as distant from her contemporaries as the star, whose name she bears, from Earth, carries an additional stigma — her foreign, German background. The philosophy she imparts to Kostoglotov embodies Kuzyomin's principle in proclaiming the primacy of spiritual values. The structure of the scene itself indicates Solzhenitsyn's intention to contact Kostoglotov from afar. When Vega talks to Kostoglotov, he does not see her, but rather watches the reflection on the ceiling of another celestial body, the sun.

The messages of Shulubin and Oreshchenkov, both teachers and representatives of a vanished epoch detached from society and ready to depart, are about all that they contribute to the theme, but their roles in the novel are quite different. Shulubin is in the mainstream of the narrative, whereas the chapter dealing with Oreshchenkov, rather artificially attached to the text, suggests that Solzhenitsyn is intentionally introducing those figures who, while remote in one way or another from the main characters, exercise a powerful influence on them.

Social distance may best be illustrated by Spiridon's relationship with Nerzhin in *The First Circle*. Spiridon's message is actually expressed by the proverb: "The wolfhound is right, and the cannibal is wrong."[14] As Kuzyomin's message reaches the reader from the remote past, so does Spiridon's reach the protagonist from an alien social and cultural stratum. Solzhenitsyn emphasizes the social and cultural distance between Spiridon and Nerzhin in the description of the latter's intricate struggle to win Spiridon's confidence and friendship and so overcome the enormous historical schism between the educated and the lower classes in Russia. As Kuzyomin is purposely endowed with superior awareness and exceptional power, Spiridon embodies the wisdom that the peasants traditionally represented to a certain part of the Russian intelligentsia. Both Kuzyomin and Spiridon articulate an ethical principle, a law in its own right. The same may be said about the concluding idea in the short story, "Matryona's House," which is inspired by a character socially and culturally distant from the narrator and at the end of the story already departed from this world.

A second distant image reflecting idealism in *The First Circle* is Kondrashov-Ivanov's painting. The ancient legend of Parsifal and the castle of the Holy Grail speaks to Nerzhin from the remote past, pointing toward spiritual aspiration and the primacy of truth and purity.

One may conclude that the recipients and donors of suppression-resisting ideas differ not only in respect to their relation to that knowledge, but also to the epoch described by Solzhenitsyn. The recipients play central roles in their respective works, whereas the common denominator of the donors is their distance, not merely from the epoch and society depicted, but also from the mainstream of Solzhenitsyn's plots.

The total effect of this pattern in Solzhenitsyn's works may seem startling. Solzhenitsyn appears to represent contemporary Soviet society as intellectually sterile, deprived of the basic human faculty of critical and creative thought. All the messages countering Stalin's propaganda stem from authoritative sources, for the most part as distant as the dictator himself. On the other hand, very few original ideas derive from the characters who are fully drawn and spotlighted and who possess neither authority nor mystery. Solzhenitsyn's protagonists form a neutral territory, an intellectual no-man's-land bombarded from the one side by Stalin's indoctrination, and from the other by messages, usually in code, opposing Stalin's ideological conditioning.

To conscience and heroism, the two main defenses against totalitarian oppression, a third faculty may now be added — human sensibility, a fine ear and sensitive vision that enable the central characters to perceive barely noticeable signals from another medium. Thus the intellectual faculties of the recipients are of little importance, and their development of the emancipating ideas they receive is virtually nil. They accept these messages almost as dogma, as divine revelations subject neither to analysis nor elaboration. Kuzyomin's code is such a message; Shukhov's brief and partial disavowal of it impresses the reader much less than the fact that Kuzyomin, after eight years, is quoted verbatim, as if his statement had been recorded in Holy Scripture. This pattern of unquestioned messages, such as Tolstoy's, Shulubin's, Oreshchenkov's and Vega's messages in *The Cancer Ward* and the letters of Volodin's mother and Spiridon's principle in *The First Circle,* recurs in most of Solzhenitsyn's works. The authoritative tone of these messages is one of Solzhenitsyn's principal idiosyncrasies: as a result of the donors' distance and mystery, the messages become a kind of absolute, religious truth; in turn, they transform the donors into oracles who must be trusted unconditionally. Thus does knowledge become faith.

Precisely this is perhaps the main difference between Solzhenitsyn and the great nineteenth-century Russian authors, especially Tolstoy, whose characters do, of course, receive signals of truth from highly unexpected sources. These messages, however, generally initiate a lengthy and usually complex intellectual as well as spiritual search for the solution to philosophical or religious dilemmas. Unfortunately, this type of intellectual seems to have vanished from contemporary Russia, at least as Solzhenitsyn presents it. In the USSR, the quest for truth and a profound understanding of the world seem to have been supplanted by the search for a new authority in which to believe and a new code of morality by which to abide. Since these new ideas contradict the ideology of the power structure, conscience, heroism, and a fine perceptivity typify Solzhenitsyn's principal characters.

Seen from this angle, two important characters in *The First Circle* assume new significance. Rubin and Sologdin, the most eloquent convicts in Sharashka who often argue heatedly, at first glance resemble old-fashioned Russian intellectuals who would spend the whole night disputing abstract topics. However, it is precisely these two characters who receive no emancipating, cognitive signals. Their role in the novel is hopelessly sinister. Their brilliance, potential, and remarkable eloquence are squandered — in one case on a ridiculous linguistic game and in the other on equally pointless research in Indo-European linguistics, both of which projects are linked to the abuse of language. Furthermore, both Rubin and Sologdin end up serving the oppressive regime, augmenting Stalin's power, and compromising themselves. The forthright condemnation of sterile intellectualism so clearly expressed through these two characters, their spiritual degeneration expressed in their collaboration with Stalin's suppressive system, contrast sharply with the religious coloration of the interactions between the donors and recipients of emancipating ideas. Thus one may conclude that Solzhenitsyn questions the validity of an independent, intellectual search for truth and that he sees no need for creative thinking in order to discover a way out of the historical tragedy of his country. All that is required is a refined perception to receive the signals from distant authorities, the acceptance of these messages on faith, and then religious, heroic adherence to their principles. Thus, regardless of whether Solzhenitsyn's characters worship Stalin or condemn him, they seem incapable of living without a religion, without some higher authority.

Thus we may wonder whether Solzhenitsyn's characters strive for freedom at all. The ancient Russian concept expressed by the noun *volja,* meaning absolute freedom and usually ascribed in folklore to the wind, the eagle, or a lonely horseman on the boundless steppe, is entirely alien to Solzhenitsyn's characters. However, even the more modest aspirations of the prerevolutionary Russian toward *svoboda,* the relative freedom of the citizen, do not attract Solzhenitsyn's protagonists. Their ideals lie in another sphere and are totally different from those of the West. They seek a new authority, perhaps stern and demanding, but fair, one that they can trust, and perhaps worship again.

# Notes and References

## Chapter One

1. In Russia, a child lacking even one parent is called an orphan.

2. *Aleksander Solzhenitsyn: Critical Essays and Documentary Materials,* John B. Dunlop, Richard Haugh, Alexis Klimoff, eds. (Belmont, Mass.: Nordland Publishing Co., 1973), p. 459.

3. Zhores A. Medvedev, *Ten Years After Ivan Denisovich* (New York: 1973), p. 28.

4. *Aleksander Solzhenitsyn: Critical Essays...,* op. cit., p. 461. "MVD" and "MGB" are abbreviations for secret police organizations.

5. Zhores A. Medvedev, *op. cit.,* pp. 199–200.

6. One must remember, of course, that it is literature which for various historical reasons traditionally served exactly these purposes in prerevolutionary Russia.

7. Alexander Solzhenitsyn: *Nobel Lecture,* F.D. Reeve, trans. (New York: Farrar, Strauss and Giroux, 1972), pp. 32–33.

8. It was published on March 3, 1974, in *The London Times,* and in abridged form in *The New York Times.* Later the document appeared as *Letter to the Soviet Leaders* (New York: Harper & Row, 1974).

## Chapter Two

1. The title of this novel was originally *One Day in the Life of a Zek.* Alexander Tvardovsky, the editor of *Novy mir,* suggested the change in title to emphasize the importance of the main character.

2. Alexander Solzhenitsyn, *One Day in the Life of Ivan Denisovich,* R. Hingley and M. Hayward, trans. (New York: Bantam, 1963), p. 100.

3. *Ibid.,* p. 17.

4. *Ibid.,* p. 94.

5. *Ibid.,* p. 170.

6. *Ibid.,* pp. 169-70.

7. *Ibid.,* p. 54.

8. *Ibid.,* pp. 66–67. The translators render the Russian word *brigada* as "gang" and *brigadir* as "boss." These words can be rendered in English more accurately as "brigade" and "foreman" respectively. In subsequent quotations these words are inserted in brackets.

9. *Ibid.,* p. 103.

10. *Ibid.*, p. 50.

11. *Ibid.*

12. *Ibid.*, p. 42.

13. *Ibid.*, p. 135.

14. *Ibid.*, p. 38.

15. *Ibid.*, p. 187.

16. *Ibid.*, p. 1.

17. *Ibid.*

18. *Ibid.*, p. 6. The translation, "Comrade Warden," is incorrect. In the USSR a convict does not have the right to address anyone with the Party title "comrade," but must use the word "citizen."

19. *Ibid.*, p. 2.

20. *Ibid.*,

21. *Ibid.* This is a more literal translation of the text.

22. *Ibid.*, pp. 78-9.

23. *Ibid.*, p. 69.

24. *Ibid.* (My translation.)

25. *Ibid.*, p. 178.

26. *Ibid.*

27. *Ibid.*, p. 202.

28. *Ibid.*, p. 195. (My translation.)

29. *Ibid.*, p. 197.

30. *Ibid.*, p. 199.

31. *Ibid.*, p. 150.

## Chapter Three

1. Alexander Solzhenitsyn, *The Cancer Ward,* Nicholas Bethell and David Burg, trans. (New York: Bantam, 1969), p. 101.

2. *Ibid.*, p. 102.

3. *Ibid.*

4. *Ibid.*

5. *Ibid.*, p. 128-29. Korchagin is a character from Nikolai Ostrovski's *How the Steel Was Tempered.* Matrosov was a hero of World War II who threw himself on a German machine gun absorbing the bullets himself.

6. *Ibid.*, p. 130.

7. *Ibid.*, p. 131.

8. *Ibid.*, p. 103.

9. *Ibid.*, p. 104.

10. *Ibid.*

11. *Ibid.*

12. *Ibid.*, p. 133, 135. A more accurate translation would be "Dissolve."

13. *Ibid.*, p. 135.

14. *Ibid.*

15. *Ibid.*, pp. 135–36.
16. *Ibid.*, p. 137.
17. *Ibid.*, p. 128.
18. *Ibid.*, p. 200.
19. *Ibid.*
20. *Ibid.*, p. 103.
21. *Ibid.*, p. 378.
22. *Ibid.*, p. 379.
23. *Ibid.*, p. 443.
24. *Ibid.*, pp. 389-90.
25. *Ibid.*, p. 276.
26. *Ibid.*, p. 279.
27. *Ibid.*, p. 319.
28. *Ibid.*, p. 317.
29. *Ibid.*, p. 451–52.
30. *Ibid.*, pp. 88–89.
31. *Ibid.*, p. 379.
32. *Ibid.*, p. 428.
33. *Ibid.*, pp. 482–83. The line Shulubin whispers is from Pushkin's poem, "Monument," written August 21, 1836, less than half a year before his death.
34. *Ibid.*, p. 335.
35. *Ibid.*, pp. 332-33.
36. *Ibid.*, pp. 333–34.
37. *Ibid.*, p. 335.
38. *Ibid.*, p. 506.
39. *Ibid.*, p. 411.
40. *Ibid.*, p. 507.
41. *Ibid.*, p. 520.
42. *Ibid.*, pp. 394–95.
43. *Ibid.*, pp. 489–90.
44. *Ibid.*, p. 434.
45. *Ibid.*, p. 440.
46. *Ibid.*, p. 442.
47. *Ibid.*, p. 203.

## Chapter Four

1. Alexander Solzhenitsyn, *The First Circle,* Thomas P. Whitney, trans. (New York: Harper & Row, 1968), p. 8.
2. *Ibid.*, p. 9.
3. *Ibid.*, p. 508.
4. *Ibid.*, p. 1.
5. *Ibid.*, p. 86.
6. *Ibid.*

7. *Ibid.*, pp. 101–02.

8. *Ibid.*, p. 111.

9. Alexander Solzhenitsyn, *The Cancer Ward*, p. 506.

10. *Ibid.*, p. 314.

11. Solzhenitsyn, *The First Circle*, p. 111.

12. *Ibid.*, pp. 111–12.

13. *Ibid.*, p. 102.

14. *Ibid.*, p. 25.

15. *Ibid.*, pp. 172–73.

16. *Ibid.*, p. 87.

17. *Ibid.*, pp. 360–61.

18. *Ibid.*, p. 476.

19. *Ibid.*, p. 262.

20. My translation.

21. *Ibid.*, p. 239.

22. *Ibid.*, p. 240.

23. *Ibid.*, pp. 557–58.

24. A paraphrase of an excerpt from a poem by Pushkin that Shulubin quotes in *The Cancer Ward*.

25. The model Solzhenitsyn used for Sologdin is Dmitri Panin, who has since emigrated from the USSR and has published *Zapiski Sologdina* (Sologdin's Notes) (Frankfurt-on-Main, Possev-Verlag, 1973). Panin's recollections of life in Sharashka corroborate the account given in *The First Circle* except that Panin vigorously disputes Solzhenitsyn's version of the manner in which Sologdin wins his freedom.

26. Solzhenitsyn, *The First Circle*, pp. 458–59.

27. *Ibid.*, p. 459.

28. *Ibid.*, p. 43.

29. *Ibid.*, p. 225.

30. *Ibid.*, p. 500.

31. *Ibid.*

32. *Ibid.*, p. 83.

33. *Ibid.*, p. 116.

34. *Ibid.*, p. 401.

35. *Ibid.*, p. 108.

### *Chapter Five*

1. Alexander Solzhenitsyn, *Stories and Prose Poems,* Michael Glenny, trans. (New York: Farrar, Straus & Giroux, 1971), p. 24.

2. *Ibid.*

3. *Ibid.*, p. 52.

4. *Ibid.*, p. 239.

5. *Ibid.*, p. 238.

6. *Ibid.*, p. 181.

7. *Ibid.*
8. *Ibid.,* p. 182.
9. *Ibid.*
10. *Ibid.*
11. *Ibid.,* pp. 182–83.
12. *Ibid.,* p. 183.
13. *Ibid.*
14. *Ibid.*
15. *Ibid.,* pp. 172–73.
16. *Ibid.,* p. 173.
17. *Ibid.,* p. 176.
18. *Ibid.,* pp. 95–96.
19. *Ibid.,* p. 110.
20. *Ibid.,* p. 114. "Strong-willed" is mistranslated as "vuluntarist" in the English text.
21. *Ibid.,* p. 113.
22. *Ibid.,* p. 111.
23. *Ibid.,* p. 116.
24. *Ibid.,* pp. 117–18.
25. *Ibid.,* p. 123.
26. My translation. In Russian, Mikheyich and Eugene's threats are not so close lexically as they appear in the English translations. Nevertheless, their meaning and emotional impact are nearly identical.
27. *Ibid.,* p. 164.
28. *Ibid.,* p. 127.

## Chapter Six

1. Alexander Solzhenitsyn, *The Love-Girl and the Innocent,* Nicholas Bethell and David Burg, trans. (New York: Bantam, 1971), p. 56.
2. *Ibid.,* p. ix.
3. My translation.
4. Solzhenitsyn, *The Love-Girl and the Innocent,* p. 87.
5. *Ibid.*
6. *Ibid.,* p. 110.

## Chapter Seven

1. Alexander Solzhenitsyn, *August 1914,* Michael Glenny, trans. (New York: Bantam, 1974), pp. 281–82.
2. My translation.
3. *August 1914,* p. 566.
4. George Kennan, "Between Earth and Hell," *The New York Review of Books,* (March 21, 1974), p. 3.
5. Alexander Solzhenitsyn, *The Gulag Archipelago,* I-II, Thomas P. Whitney, trans. (New York: Harper & Row, 1973), p. 284. My translation.

## Chapter Eight

1. Solzhenitsyn's term, *zek,* for example, derives from an abbreviation of the Russian word for convict: *zakliuchennyi,* an adjectival noun in the masculine singular form. This abbreviation existed in the Russian language for years and was written *zeka,* a word derived from the sounds of two letters of the Russian alphabet pronounced respectively *zeh* and *kah.* However, since Russian nouns ending in *a* (with a few exceptions) are of feminine gender, while the noun "convict" in Russian is masculine and usually refers to a man, the discrepancy between the grammatical and the actual genders created an abstraction. Solzhenitsyn modified this old acronym very effectively by dropping the final *a* sound and thus writing *zek.* The term immediately changes gender, since Russian nouns ending in a hard consonant are masculine. As a result, Solzhenitsyn's monosyllabic masculine noun *zek,* of the same gender as the person it names, begins to behave like a noun and thus loses its direct relationship with its root word *zakliuchennyi.* In addition, the masculine *-ek* ending, rather rare in Russian, is immediately associated with the few nouns with this ending. Among them, the most semantically appropriate is *chelovek,* meaning "human being." Thus the term becomes personified, humanized. It is a new name, no longer humiliating, referring to a member of the nation living on the islands of the Gulag Archipelago.

In the third part of *The Gulag Archipelago* (not discussed in this study, since it was published after Solzhenitsyn's expulsion from the USSR) the author acknowledges that the term *zek* is not his own invention. Nevertheless, he was the first to introduce it in a literary context with the above-described semantic and esthetic effects.

2. In the third part of *The Gulag Archipelago,* Solzhenitsyn comments on the problem of compassion as treated in literature by authors from different social classes. His discourse on the subject, however, seems simplistic and totally unconvincing.

3. *Cancer Ward,* p. 66.

4. *Ibid.,* p. 205.

5. Leo Tolstoy, *War and Peace,* Leo Wiener, trans. (New York: Colonial Press, 1904), Vol. IV, p. 88.

6. Alexander Solzhenitsyn, *August 1914,* Michael Glenny, trans. (New York: Bantam, 1974), p. 369.

7. *Cancer Ward,* p. 204.

8. *The First Circle,* p. 566.

9. *Ibid.,* p. 3.

10. Faddey is called Ilya in the English translation.

11. *Cancer Ward,* p. 444.

12. *The First Circle,* p. 489 (my translation).

13. This chapter was published in the emigré magazine *Kontinent,* 1, 1974.

14. *The First Circle,* p. 401.

# Selected Bibliography

PRIMARY SOURCES

SOLZHENITSYN, ALEXANDER, *August 1914,* trans. by Michael Glenny. New York: Bantam Books, 1974.

———, *The Cancer Ward,* trans. by Nicholas Bethell and David Burg. New York: Bantam Books, 1969.

———, *The First Circle,* trans. by Thomas P. Whitney. New York: Harper & Row, 1968.

———, *The Gulag Archipelago,* trans. by Thomas P. Whitney. New York: Harper & Row, 1973.

———, *Letter to the Soviet Leaders,* trans. by Hilary Sternberg. New York: Harper & Row, 1974.

———, *The Love-Girl and the Innocent,* trans. by Nicholas Bethell and David Burg. New York: Bantam Books, 1971.

———, *Nobel Lecture,* trans. by F.D. Reeve. New York: Farrar, Straus and Giroux, 1972.

———, *One Day in the Life of Ivan Denisovich,* trans. by Max Hayward and Ronald Hingley. New York: Bantam Books, 1963.

———, *Stories and Prose Poems,* trans. by Michael Glenny. New York: Farrar, Straus and Giroux, 1970.


SECONDARY SOURCES

LUKÁCS, GEORG, *Solzhenitsyn.* trans. by William David Graf. Cambridge, Mass.: MIT Press, 1971. A study concerned not so much with Solzhenitsyn's works *per se* as with the development of "social realism."

MEDVEDEV, ZHORES A., *Ten Years after Ivan Denisovich.* New York: Alfred A. Knopf, 1973. A book with extremely important insights and thorough documentation.

MOODY, CHRISTOPHER, *Solzhenitsyn.* New York: Harper & Row, Publishers, Perennial Library, 1973. A summary of Solzhenitsyn's major works.

ROTHBERG, ABRAHAM, *Aleksandr Solzhenitsyn: The Major Novels.* Ithaca, N.Y.: Cornell University Press, 1971. An attempt to evaluate the political impact of Solzhenitsyn's principal works.

*Solzhenitsyn — A Documentary Record,* ed. by LEOPOLD LABEDZ. New York: Harper & Row, 1971. A thorough and reliable documentation of the Solzhenitsyn affair.

1. General Background

GIBIAN, GEORGE, *Interval of Freedom: Soviet Literature during the Thaw 1954-1957.* Minneapolis: University of Minnesota Press, 1960. An excellent introduction to the literature of the period of relative freedom in the Soviet Union. Essential for every reader of Solzhenitsyn's works who wishes to place them in the correct historical perspective.

MOORE, HARRY T. and ALBERT PARRY, *Twentieth-Century Russian Literature.* Carbondale, Illinois: Southern Illinois University Press, 1974. A very concise, rather schematic work. See especially the last two chapters, "The Forbidden Ones" and "Anatomy of Dissent."

2. Critical and Biographical Studies

*Aleksandr Solzhenitsyn: Critical Essays and Documentary Materials.* Ed. by JOHN B. DUNLOP, RICHARD HAUGH, and ALEXIS KLIMOFF. Belmont, Mass.: Nordland, 1973. A varied, well-edited collection of studies on Solzhenitsyn. The volume contains excellent translations of Solzhenitsyn's public statements and an annotated bibliography.

BJÖRKEGREN, HANS, *Aleksandr Solzhenitsyn.* Trans. by Kaarina Eneberg. New York: The Third Press, 1972. One of the first serious attempts to compile Solzhenitsyn's biography.

BURG, DAVID and GEORGE FEIFER, *Solzhenitsyn.* New York: Stein and Day, 1973. A highly speculative biography of Solzhenitsyn incorporating details from the writer's works.

*Canadian Slavonic Papers,* Vol. XIII, No. 2 & 3, Summer-Fall, 1971. Contains several critical works on Solzhenitsyn's fiction and his style.

KENNAN, GEORGE, "Between Earth and Hell," *The New York Review,* March 21, 1974. A brilliant review of *The Gulag Archipelago* (Parts I and II) with excellent political and philosophical comments.

# Index

The Works of Solzhenitsyn are listed under his name. The names of the characters in Solzhenitsyn's works are listed as they occur most frequently in this book.

## DATE DUE

| | | | |
|---|---|---|---|
| | | | |
| | | | |
| | | | |
| | | | |
| | | | |
| | | | |
| | | | |
| | | | |
| | | | |
| | | | |
| | | | |